Edwin Gaston Collins

Buy the Truth and Sell it Not:
The Life of E. Gaston Collins

Frank N. Cook

Unclouded Press
Lewisburg, Tennessee

Copyright © MMXIV by Frank N. Cook
All rights reserved.

ISBN 978 0 9912785 0 3 (Library binding)
ISBN 978 0 9912785 1 0 (Softcover)
ISBN 978 0 9912785 2 7 (Digital edition)

Library of Congress Control Number: 2014904040

Library of Congress Subject Headings:
Churches of Christ--Biography.
Tennessee, Middle--History.
Churches of Christ--Doctrines.
Education--Maritime Provinces--History.
Churches of Christ--Ontario--History.

BISAC Subject Heading:
BIO018000 BIOGRAPHY & AUTOBIOGRAPHY / Religious

BIC Subject Category: BGX Biography: religious & spiritual

Cover Art © Nancy S. Hilgert
http://www.fineartbynancyhilgert.com

Published in Tennessee, the greenest state in the land of the free, in the United States of America. Printing location is indicated on the final page.

Section I – Dear Hearts and Gentle People
Chapter 1 - Beans Creek --------------------------- p. 1
Chapter 2 - The Matriarch ---------------------- p. 5
Chapter 3 - Old Salem ----------------------------- p. 15
Chapter 4 - De Troubles of de World ----------- p. 21
Chapter 5 - The Iron Horse ---------------------- p. 26

Section II – O Canada!
Chapter 6 - The Remarkable Tallmans ---------- p. 33
Chapter 7 - College Years------------------------ p. 37
Chapter 8 - Ada ---------------------------------- p. 43
Chapter 9 - The Attack --------------------------- p. 46

Section III – The Evangelist
Chapter 10 - Survival----------------------------- p. 52
Chapter 11 - Algood, Lipscomb and Bridgeport- p. 58
Chapter 12 - Meaford by the Bay ----------------- p. 69
Chapter 13 - The Editor -------------------------- p. 75
Chapter 14 - The Father -------------------------- p. 79
Chapter 15 - Back to the States ------------------ p. 82

Section IV – Sell it Not
Chapter 16 - Warfare ----------------------------- p.100
Chapter 17 - The Prayer -------------------------- p.104
Chapter 18 - All Be One -------------------------- p.113

Section V – The Light Shines in Darkness
Chapter 19 - Going Home ------------------------- p.118
Chapter 20 - The Unclouded Day ----------------- p.129

Endnotes-- p.132
Illustrations ------------------------------------ p.143
Bibliography-------------------------------------- p.149

Appendices

A – My Last Railway Journey ---------------------- p.153
  by E. Gaston Collins
  from his high school composition book, c.1908.

B – Autobiography of Claire Collins --------------- p.155
  a school assignment when she was a junior in high
  school in Portland, Tennessee in 1930.

C – Unequal Yoking -------------------------------- p.165
  or "Be Not Unequally Yoked With Unbelievers,"
  being a treatise on the relationship of the Christian
  to the world, by E. Gaston Collins, 1924.

D – Does it Pay to Go to Church? ------------------ p.191
  a handout for the Radnor Church of Christ
  by E. Gaston Collins, 1935.

E – List of Songs from "Song Hints" -------------- p.193
  by E. Gaston Collins in *Around the Lord's Table,*
  Gospel Advocate Company, 1934.

F – To Read the Entire Bible in Twelve Months-- p.196
  by E. Gaston Collins, 1943.

G – Who Were the "Very Chiefest Apostles?"----- p.200
  by E. Gaston Collins, *Word and Work,* 1955.

H – Hot A-Plenty by Now (Or, A Rather Rude
  Disillusionment) by E. Gaston Collins, 1955. - p.205

I – Memos on The Collins Cemetery Association p.212
  by E. Gaston Collins, 1966.

Acknowledgements

The contributions of many people made this work possible, including:
- my "favorite aunt," Verna Thompson,
- my sister-by-marriage, Pat Cook,
- my niece, Alison Cook,
- my siblings: Jane George, David Cook and Billy Cook;
- my cousin, Barbara Arledge,
- Geoffrey Ellis and Paul Linn Dale of the Canadian Churches of Christ Historical Society,
- Jerry Limbaugh and Judy Phillips of the Franklin County, TN Historical Society,
- Marie Byers of the Lipscomb University Beaman Library Special Collections,
- Neil Anderson of the *Gospel Advocate*,
- Larry Miles of *Word and Work*,
- Buddy Reynolds of Old Salem Church of Christ,
- Cheryl Cole of Winchester, TN,
- Amelia Pettes of Robertson Fork Church of Christ,
- my daughter, Rachel Cook who gave English advice,
- and my dear mother, Claire Cook, who left letters, clippings, photographs and memories.

The help of all these people has been absolutely essential, but the responsibility for all opinions expressed and for any mistakes made is all mine.

Finally, I owe a debt of gratitude to my granddaddy, E. Gaston Collins, whose writings, letters, and photographs made it easy for this amateur biographer, and whose life of integrity inspires me to buy the truth, and sell it not.

Frank N. Cook

Buy the truth, and sell it not.
- Proverbs 23:23

Section I

Dear Hearts and Gentle People

Buy the Truth and Sell it Not

Chapter 1
Beans Creek

At least two of his great-great-great grandfathers fought in the American Revolution. His great-great grandfather was a hero at the Battle of New Orleans. His grandfather rode with the cavalry in the War Between the States. For E. Gaston Collins, however, life would be about spiritual, rather than carnal warfare.

He was born December 4, 1890 to Jim and Lizzie Collins in Franklin County, Tennessee near Beans Creek. The area around Beans Creek had been settled shortly after Tennessee became a state in 1796. The first member of the Bean family in the Tennessee territory was William Bean, who settled on the Watauga River in east Tennessee. His sons established Beans Station in Grainger County. After the defeat of many of the hostile Indians at Nickajack in 1795, settlers began streaming into middle Tennessee. Among them was Jesse Bean, who in 1800 settled along the creek that now bears his name.[1]

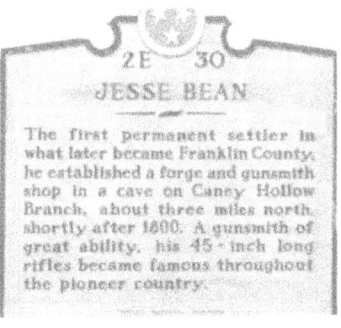

Beans Creek flows through the fertile rolling fields of the Highland Rim that surrounds middle Tennessee. Even today, many plant nurseries are located in the area because of the favorable growing conditions. The growing of cotton quickly became a major industry, and slaves were brought in to help run the small farms. Corn, grain, potatoes and tobacco all became cash crops as well. The

Buy the Truth and Sell it Not

creek was navigable primarily during flood season, and brave flatboat men carried the crops to market down the creek into the Elk River, and then into the Tennessee, Ohio, and Mississippi rivers.[2]

Beans Creek community today is a small, quiet, rural residential area that shows little evidence of the thriving economy it once anchored. A county road crosses the creek near the old stagecoach line crossing. The railroad tracks, which were laid in 1858, were taken up in 1986, and the old depot is also gone.

About a mile and a half north of Beans Creek community was a stagecoach stop at Salem. It was a big event when settlers would hear the stagecoach driver blowing his bugle from a mile away to announce his impending arrival.[3] When Franklin County, Tennessee was organized in 1807, Salem was a leading community in the county. Besides the stagecoach stop, there was Jesse Bean's gun shop and powder mill, a Baptist church begun in 1812, grist mills started by Jacob Rich and George Stovall, a cotton gin, and a still house.[4] Falls Mill, about a mile north of Salem, was built as a textile mill in 1873 and later changed to a grain mill. It is still operating today.[5]

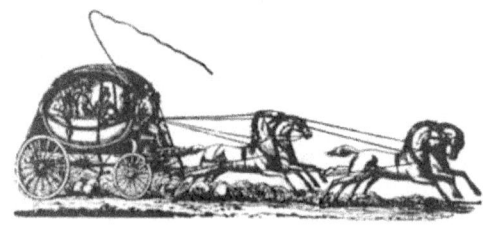

A Nashville newspaper in 1828 stated, "The village of Salem is situated in the county of Franklin, in a wealthy and populous neighborhood, surrounded by a body of land as fertile as any in the state."[6] An 1834 publication describes Salem as "a post town in Franklin County, ninety-four miles southeast from Nashville, at the crossing

Dear Hearts and Gentle People

of Beans Creek, on the Huntsville Road."[7] Salem was growing so quickly that in 1838 Tennessee extended the corporate limits of Salem.[8]

One of the now-prominent early settlers of Franklin County was David Crockett. In the fall of 1812, he and his wife Polly settled on a farm he named "Kentuck" less than two miles east of Beans Creek.[9] Though hostile Indian tribes had been diminished in numbers, they still troubled the area. In 1812, in nearby Beech Grove, a Mrs. Tucker had gone to the spring when Indians came to her house and killed her two little boys.[10] The next year, the bloody massacre of hundreds of settlers and soldiers at Ft. Mims, Alabama prompted many from Franklin County to volunteer for the Creek Indian War, among them David Crockett.

Soon after the war, David's beloved Polly died and was buried near their homestead. By 1817, David had remarried and moved on to Lawrence County, Tennessee, headed for national fame. Crockett's Kentuck farm is today the site of a plant nursery.

Also among the early settlers in Franklin County were Archibald Woods and his son-in-law, Barbe[11] Collins, who arrived about 1809. Archibald was captain of a Virginia rifleman militia in the American Revolution[12] and had a land grant, probably for his service in the war.[13] Archibald's six brothers had also served in the war, and several of them settled in Franklin County. The Woods family helped form the Salem Baptist Church.

Barbe Collins was a captain in the 1st Regiment of the West Tennessee Militia from November 13, 1814 till May 13, 1815. Captain Collins, who was Gaston Collins great-great grandfather, has a tombstone[14] inscribed "One of the

Buy the Truth and Sell it Not

Barbe Collins

heroes of New Orleans." No doubt he was in the thick of the fighting when the Redcoats charged, for twelve of his eighty-five men died in the service.[15] Some of the deaths may have come from disease in the camps, along with the battle fatalities.

One of the original explorers of Franklin County, along with Jesse Bean, was John Hunt, who gave his name to Huntsville, Alabama. His son, David Hunt, settled in Franklin County and had a son named Clinton Armstrong Hunt in 1808. In the 1850's, the residents of Salem didn't want the railroad coming through their town, so Clinton Hunt offered his land.[16] The railroad came, and in 1860 a post office was established at Hunt's Station, later called Hunt, then Huntland. Huntland is about a mile and a half southwest of the Beans Creek community.

The people who settled Franklin County were strong, hard-working, brave and God-fearing. Many, many years later, when the popular singer Dinah Shore sang about the "Dear hearts and gentle people who live in my hometown," she no doubt had in mind the hard-working, God-fearing people of her native Franklin County, Tennessee.[17]

Dear Hearts and Gentle People

Chapter 2
The Matriarch

Ann Day Lipscomb

The family of William Lipscomb arrived in Franklin County about 1826. William was born in 1774 in Spotsylvania County, Virginia[18] (the Fredericksburg area). Ann Day Cooke was born in 1779 in Louisa County, Virginia (the next county to the southeast). Ann's father,

Buy the Truth and Sell it Not

William Cooke, was a veteran of the American Revolution, having served in the 1st Artillery Regiment of Continental troops.[19] After the war, he became a preacher at the Little River Baptist Church in Louisa County. William Cooke performed the ceremony when Ann Cooke and William Lipscomb were married in December 1796 in Louisa County.[20]

William and Ann were middle-aged with many children when they decided to move to Franklin County, probably seeking better lives for their children. In 1828, William bought 468 acres just west of Beans Creek for $3740. He and Ann began to build a brick house of seven rooms resembling the architecture of Tidewater, Virginia.[21] They named their house Mt. Airy.[22] The ruins of the house still stand today[23], but William likely never saw its completion. On his 55th birthday, January 17, 1829, he was killed by a falling tree.

With the death of her husband, responsibility for the house and the farm fell to Ann and her sons, William, Granville, Dabney, and John. By all accounts, Ann had a strong character and constitution. She seldom rode, but usually walked wherever she went. On Sunday, she walked the two miles to church in Salem. A picture of one of Ann's daughters, Frances Cooke Lipscomb Van Zandt, perhaps gives us a glimpse of how Ann may have looked in her younger days.

Frances Van Zandt

Dear Hearts and Gentle People

Ann was very involved with her large family. Each census shows family members, often grandchildren, living in the same house with her. At one point she had four grandsons in Tolbert Fanning's Franklin College, and at least once she sent them a package which included, among other things, a twenty dollar gold piece to be divided among them.[24]

With the approach of the Civil War, Tennessee, like the rest of the country, had divided opinions. There were pockets of Union support and pockets of Secessionists, and there were pockets of people who just wanted to be left alone. Franklin County was a strong secessionist area. When Tennessee first voted to reject secession on February 6, 1861, many citizens of Franklin County met on the courthouse square and decided the county would secede from the state of Tennessee and petition Alabama to let them join them in the Confederacy.[25] Before any action could be taken, however, the battle of Ft. Sumter occurred, and Lincoln called for troops to invade the South. Tennessee quickly changed her mind and voted June 8 to secede.

Several of the Lipscomb family joined the Confederate Army, and Ann lost two grandsons in the war. William Lipscomb's son Ira died at the battle of Petersburg, Virginia.[26] Dr. Thomas Lipscomb's son Willie rode in Forrest's escort. He died at the age of 18 in action near Mt Pleasant, Tennessee.[27] Goodspeeds History of Tennessee says that Ann Day Lipscomb knit over 100 pairs of socks for Confederate soldiers during the war.[28]

Union troop movements in the area of Salem began as early as May 1862.[29] The area swarmed with troops after the battle of Stones River as General Rosecrans assaulted Tullahoma before moving on to Chattanooga. The rail line and stagecoach road through Salem guaranteed it would be part of Rosecrans' movements. Some of Sherman's troops also passed through Salem on their way to Chattanooga. The Union Provost Marshal in charge of keeping order among civilians had several reports charging Ann's son William Lipscomb and daughter-in-law Jane Lipscomb with being disloyal and aiding bushwhackers.[30]

Granville Lipscomb's son John married Annie Smith. Her father was visited by Yankees at his home in Beans Creek. Told that there was no food on the place, the soldiers went to the slave quarters, where they were told that Smith had hams and bacon hidden in the attic. Returning to the house, they found the goods, led Smith out of the house and killed him.[31]

In Ann Day Lipscomb's obituary, her grandson said that Sherman's men came to her house on her 84th birthday and cleaned out everything she owned. It's possible he had the wrong date, because on Ann's birthday, August 8, 1863, Sherman's men were still in Vicksburg, where they had just completed the starvation of that city. Some of Sherman's army did pass through Salem a little later, leaving Vicksburg in late September and arriving in Bridgeport, Alabama on the 15th of November.[32]

It's also possible that every evil deed at the time was attributed to Sherman. There were other Yankees passing Ann's house in August 1863. General McCook, serving under Rosecrans, moved part of his men from Decherd through Salem on the way to Stevenson, Alabama that August.[33] It's also possible that Rosecrans and Sherman both looted Ann's house.

Dear Hearts and Gentle People

Whoever did the looting, the result was the same: everything of value was stolen from the house. From that day till Ann's death six years later, she lived with her daughter Tahpenes (Tappie) Lipscomb Hunt, the wife of Clinton Armstrong Hunt. After her death, her estate filed a claim with the Federal government for repayment of the items stolen from her house. It was, like most Southern claims, denied.[34]

Ann Day Lipscomb had such a commanding presence that even her three year old great-grandson remembered her many years later. W.L. Moore, writing in 1946, recalled her visits while he was a toddler, "They used to bring her to our house from the front gate in a chair, and she would sit by the big woodfire in my mother's room by the north window."[35]

After Ann passed, her body was laid to rest next to her husband William near their old homeplace. Though the house is vacant and gutted today, sitting in the middle of a cow lot with a barn attached, it still has a quiet strength and beauty about it that is a testament to the original owners.

Mt. Airy

Buy the Truth and Sell it Not

Ann's tombstone reads, "Bleessed are the dead that die in the lord, that thay may rest from thier labours."

Ann D. Lipscomb

No better tributes to Gaston Collins great-great grandmother Ann Day Lipscomb can be found than those composed in 1870 by her grandchildren Annie Moore and David Lipscomb, reprinted with permission of the *Gospel Advocate*.[36]

Hunt's Station, Tenn., March 27th, 1870.

Dear Cousin David: Our dear old grandmother, Ann Day Lipscomb, was consigned to the grave, at her old homestead, this Lordsday afternoon. At eight o'clock yesterday morning, she yielded without a struggle to the embraces of that silent slumber that knows no waking on earth.

I presume an obituary by you will be expected, and will doubtless be of interest to many of your readers. She

Dear Hearts and Gentle People

was born August 8th, 1778, and was at the time of her death 91 years, 7 months and 18 days old.

She was, as you know, the mother of eleven children, of fifty-six grandchildren, and seventy-six great-grandchildren. I will say nothing more to one who has known her from his earliest recollection.

Affectionately, Annie Moore

The maiden name of the above was Ann D. Cook. She was the daughter of Elder Wm. Cook, a Baptist preacher of Louisa county, Va. She was married in early youth to Wm. Lipscomb. The necessities of a large family induced them to emigrate to the cheaper and more fertile lands of Tennessee, in the year 1826. About two years after their removal, her husband was killed by the falling of a tree. The responsibilities of a large family in a land of strangers were thrown upon her. These heavy responsibilities only served to develop fully her quiet strength of will, her calm, modest self-reliance, her sound, discriminating judgement, her wonderful energy and untiring perseverance. She was industrious and economical in her habits, frugal and simple in her tastes. She was a good careful provider preserving and husbanding what she made. Her home, while a model of old fashioned simplicity, always abounded with plenty, which was dispensed with unstinted hospitality. She was fond of her friends, her relatives, and especially fond of children and loved to have them with her. She raised from infancy to womanhood, three generations of her family. Her home was always the fond resort of her large family of children, grand-children and great-grand-children.

She lived in the enjoyment of remarkable strength of mind and body, supervising her own affairs, doing her own housework and chiefly her own cooking, until 84 years of age. Her home had about this time been

Buy the Truth and Sell it Not

subject, as all other homes in her country were, to the pillaging and marauding parties of Sherman's army. On her 84th birthday, although she was unable to be out of bed, the house was entirely stripped of all that years of industrious economy had provided, and not enough for a single meal for herself left in the house. Her youngest daughter, Mrs. Tahpenes Hunt, on the afternoon of the same day, carried her from her old home, to which she never returned, until she returned to sleep the sleep of death, beside a large family of her descendents that had already preceded her to the grave. After her removal from her old home she was kindly and tenderly cared for in the house of her son-in-law, C.A. Hunt. Her physical and mental powers soon began to rapidly fail, but she relapsed into a happy state of second childhood, enjoying more than aught else, the companionship and amusements of her great-grandchildren.

She, in early life, became religious, and united with the Baptist Church at Little River, Va. On her removal to Tennessee she united with the Baptist Church at Bean's Creek, Franklin Co., Tenn. Her religion was not emotional or demonstrative, but deeply earnest and practical. When able, she was seldom absent from her place at church, habitually walking in her vigor, (she seldom ever rode), two or three miles to church and back. But religion found its purest exemplification with her in deeds of practical piety. Careful and pains-taking, she was yet liberal to the poor. A case of want or suffering in her reach never went unaided. While oft' reproving, sometimes plainly and severely, the idleness and wastefulness that brought want, she still relieved it with a generous hand. She was a kind, a good neighbor; she was careful of the comfort of all about her.

While she was partial to her own, and strong in her partialities, and loved her own kindred with a deep and earnest love, her sympathies were as wide and deep as

Dear Hearts and Gentle People

human sufferings or sorrows. When the report of the first blood shed in the late cruel strife reached her, she drew a long and deep sigh. Some one present noticing it, said: "Why, Aunt, *the killed were not our boys.*" She responded: "No, but they are somebody's boys, that will sadly mourn for them." Thus, while her feelings, from the very necessities of her nature, were with her own people, yet her sympathies went forth with tender regard to the homes and hearts of the North that were stricken with suffering and sorrow in the bitter strife.

For several years past, she has seemed especially to look forward to death with joyful and happy anticipations, eager to be at home with Christ, her Savior.

Her old, wrinkled and familiar face will be sadly missed by many hearts that loved her well. In her death the centre of affection and the bond of union in a large and continually increasing family, has been removed from earth. She had faults, weaknesses, seemingly inseparable from one of her earnest and active temperament in life. She stamped her own unpretending, laborious character and impatient temperament very largely upon her family. But she performed her part in life well. She discharged its duties in all her relationships with conscientious fidelity.

She lived far beyond the allotted years of human life in the enjoyment of unusual strength of body and mind. In old age the restless energy of her more vigorous days mellowed into a gentle, patient resignation and eager willingness to depart and be with Christ. She was free from murmuring, appreciative of every attention paid her, and contented and happy with her surroundings. She has gone to a home of happiness and peace. We humbly pray that each one of her large family may so live as to meet her in the abode of the blessed.

D. L.

Buy the Truth and Sell it Not

Old Salem Church of Christ building

Dear Hearts and Gentle People

Chapter 3
Old Salem

As a result of the Reformation Movement begun in the 16th century by Martin Luther and others, many different denominations of the church had appeared, each seeking the best way of serving God. In the 18th and 19th centuries, some people began questioning whether any denomination followed the pattern set by God. They wondered if it would be best to unite all Christians in a restoration of the New Testament church. Thus was begun the Restoration Movement.

Alexander Campbell was the best known of the men seeking to restore the church, but there were many others, from John Glas to Barton W. Stone. Out of their study and work came a number of principles of restoration, often expressed like this:

- Speak where Scriptures speak, and be silent where Scriptures are silent.
- Call Bible things by Bible names; do Bible things in Bible ways.
- No headquarters but heaven; no creed but Christ; no book but the Bible.
- In matters of faith, unity; in matters of opinion, liberty, and in all things, charity.

About 1830, Ann Day Lipscomb's son Granville began reading Alexander Campbell's publication *The Christian Baptist* and discussing it with his brothers. The minister of the Beans Creek Baptist Church, William Woods, (Gaston's great-great-great uncle) didn't like the Lipscombs reading the Bible on their own.[37] Shortly after

Buy the Truth and Sell it Not

that, Granville, Dabney, and John Lipscomb were expelled from the church for advocating the New Testament as the only rule of faith and practice.[38] Salem Church of Christ began with four white and five colored members in May of 1834. By Christmas of that year, the number was thirty-four whites and twelve colored.[39] In spite of their religious differences, the Woods and the Lipscombs remained friends.[40]

There are some people for whom the Word of God makes little impression on their lives. There are others who cannot live in fragments, but must connect their beliefs to actions.[41] For these people the Word of God is living and powerful and sharper than a two-edged sword.[42] Granville Lipscomb (David Lipscomb's father and Gaston Collins' great-great uncle) was one of these people. Soon after Granville began studying the Word diligently, he began to question whether or not it was right to own slaves. At the time, it was not legally possible to free your slaves in Tennessee. So, in 1835, Granville Lipscomb and two of his brothers moved their families to Sangamon County, Illinois, so they could free their slaves across the border in the Indiana territory.

The move to Illinois successfully freed the slaves, but it was disastrous for the rest of the family. Shortly after Granville bought a 320 acre farm, the temperature dropped to 19 below zero. After a hard winter, spring brought constant rain and flooding. "Fever and ague," which was an archaic name for malaria[43] claimed many lives, among them Granville's wife and three children.[44] On December 1, 1836, Granville sold his farm for the exact amount he had paid for it and returned to Tennessee with three children.[45]

Dear Hearts and Gentle People

After the return from Illinois, the Salem Church continued to grow, meeting from house to house. In 1842, Granville's mother, Ann Day Lipscomb left the Baptist church and united with the Salem Church of Christ. In 1843, it was decided to build a place of worship. Peter Simmons donated land on the waters of Beans Creek, and a meeting house was finished in 1847.[46]

During the war, Yankees occupied the church building, destroying all the furnishings, doors and windows, so that the church once again had to meet from house to house. After the war, plans were made for rebuilding. Thomas F. Mosely donated land just up the hill from the old location and a new building was begun by R.G. Henson and James Crawley in 1875. The new brick structure, 50' by 33' by 14' was completed the next year and David Lipscomb preached the first sermon in it.

David Lipscomb

This building, still in use, at first had two front doors: one for men and one for women. Men and women originally sat on opposite sides, and there were two communion cups, one for each side.[47] Today the two single doors have been combined into one double door, and all partake from one communion tray. The original podium is still in use today.

Buy the Truth and Sell it Not

The Salem Church continued to grow in spite of divisions occurring within the Restoration Movement. The principle of "No headquarters but heaven" was tested by the formation by some churches of the American Christian Missionary Society in 1849. These "digressives" were establishing an order outside of the pattern given in the New Testament, many claimed.

The Restoration principle of "In faith, unity, and in opinion, liberty" was tested by the introduction of instrumental music into some churches in 1859, with some believing it was a matter of opinion and others not. The conflicts of the War Between the States often deepened these other conflicts.[48] By the twentieth century, Salem had stopped occasionally referring to itself as Salem Christian Church or the Disciples of Christ at Salem, but called itself only Salem Church of Christ, to distinguish itself from churches using instrumental music.

One of the members of Old Salem during the late 19th century was Gaston's grandfather, William Lipscomb Collins. The 1860 census of Franklin County shows that he lived in the house with his grandmother, Ann Day Lipscomb,[49] probably because both his parents had died before he was twenty. William L. Collins attended Tolbert Fanning's Franklin College. He married Mary Jane Bickley in 1860, with his cousin David Lipscomb performing the ceremony. He became a farmer and shop-keeper,[50] and eventually owned the farm where Ann Day Lipscomb's house stood.[51]

One account that Gaston gave of a service at Old Salem Church shows that Will Collins could be fervent about his religion:

Dear Hearts and Gentle People

"Old Salem is the name of one of the oldest congregations in Franklin County, Tenn., your Editor's home county. It is the stamping ground of the Lipscombs, and many others who were instrumental in advancing the gospel, and the scene of many a happy occasion during revivals. I am told of one such occasion in the life-time of my paternal grandfather.

William Lipscomb Collins

Buy the Truth and Sell it Not

It was at a night meeting during a revival; they were standing, as usual, and singing the invitation hymn. Some seven or eight responded to the invitation to come to Jesus, among them possibly one of his sons. This sight filled his soul with joy and he mounted one of the front seats which gave his tall figure a commanding view of the audience, and shouted right out in the meeting, 'Let them all come.' I am glad my mother was there. I wish I could have been there, too. Many times I live over in memory the numerous happy associations there, and pray that there shall be a light burning at Old Salem 'till he come' again. – E.G.C."[52]

Gaston Collins would be raised in a strong church that was filled with family members, friends, and neighbors. Years later, after Gaston had left home, a preacher wrote him and said that when he visited Salem, he "was glad to see your mother present the last week of meetings. It seemed like olden times."[53] The congregation was filled with the gentle spirit of David Lipscomb[54] and others like him who sought truth and unity and brotherly love. These are the teachings in which Gaston would be nurtured.

Dear Hearts and Gentle People

Chapter 4
De Troubles of de World

The war had brought many changes to Franklin County. All the best horses, cattle, and hogs were gone, along with many personal possessions and houses. The worst loss of all, of course, was that many young men never came home.

The former slaves enjoyed their new found freedom, but many were worse off economically than before the war, simply because things were worse for everyone. A very few negroes became criminals, and often suffered harshly for it. The last known act of frontier justice in the area occurred in 1901. A negro man murdered a white woman in her home, and the community lived in fear for several days until a group of vigilantes captured the culprit and burned him alive.[55]

Some whites tried to help the former slaves. Some, such as James Campbell, gave money to help former slaves. Wallace Estill tried to create a community of freed slaves.[56] A very few former slaves did well for themselves. Dr. Michael Bradley tells the story of William Key, a slave born in 1833 and raised in Franklin County. He went to war with his two young masters and twice escaped lynching at the hands of the Yankees. After the war, he used his skills at treating animals and his skills at card-playing to make enough money to buy his former masters farm and return it to them, as well as pay for their college.[57]

For most people, there was an "equality of poverty"[58] between the races. Most blacks and whites had to put on their work boots six days a week and go to the fields to eke

Buy the Truth and Sell it Not

out an existence. In many people's hearts, there was also the belief that all were equal before God. Before the war, many whites had taken their slaves to church, but whether most slaves went willingly or by compulsion is unclear.[59] After the war, many former slaves began meeting in their own church groups. Gaston later commented on the equality of all before God, "we all are standing in the need of charity – mercy – grace – forgiveness. I've heard the negroes touchingly sing, 'Standing in the need of prayer. It's ME, O Lord! Standin' in the need of prayer.'"[60]

It's me, it's me, it's me, O Lord

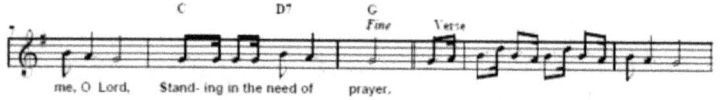

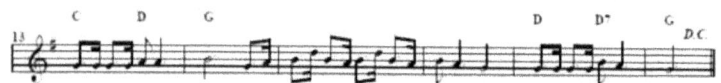

Refrain

It's me, it's me, it's me, O Lord,
Standing in the need of prayer.
It's me, it's me, it's me, O Lord,
Standing in the need of prayer.

Not my brother or my sister,
but it's me, O Lord,
Standing in the need of prayer.
Not my brother or my sister,
but it's me, O Lord,
Standing in the need of prayer.

Refrain

Not my mother or my father,
but it's me, O Lord,
Standing in the need of prayer.
Not my mother or my father,
but it's me, O Lord,
Standing in the need of prayer.

Refrain

Not the stranger or my neighbour,
but it's me, O Lord,
Standing in the need of prayer.
Not the stranger or my neighbour,
but it's me, O Lord,
Standing in the need of prayer.

Refrain

Dear Hearts and Gentle People

Gaston's other grandfather moved to Franklin County after the war. J.B. O'Neal had been born in Laurens County, South Carolina in 1836. In April 1861, he enlisted in Company F of the 3rd South Carolina infantry. Three months later, he fought in the first Battle of Bull Run. He then enlisted in Company G of the 2nd South Carolina cavalry in April 1862 and saw much action. He was wounded at Upperville, Virginia and at Gettysburg, Pennsylvania, but stayed with the cavalry until it surrendered in 1865. He carried a ball in his right hip for the rest of his life.[61] In 1869 he married Martha B. Walker of New Market, Alabama. Gaston's mother, Mary Elizabeth (Lizzie) O'Neal, was born there August 27, 1871. Shortly thereafter, the family moved across the state line to Huntland, Tennessee.

In 1884, Martha died of tuberculosis, leaving Lizzie, then twelve and the oldest girl, with much of the burden of raising her brothers and sisters. J.B. O'Neal worked as a blacksmith and later as Justice of the Peace.[62] On July 6, 1889, Lizzie, just shy of her 18th birthday, married James Monroe Collins. On Thursday, December 4 of 1890, Edwin Gaston Collins made his entrance into the world. He was soon joined by two sisters, Mollie Jane in 1894, and Willie in 1895.

The old spiritual says, "Soon I'll be done with de troubles of de world," and Gaston Collins had his share of troubles, as well as triumphs in life. Trouble began when he was age five. On November 2, 1895 his grandfather, Will Collins, who owned the farm where Gaston's family resided, died at age 61.[63] The following January 26, Gaston's father, Jim Collins died at age 31 of a nosebleed.

As she had at age twelve, Lizzie Collins once again shouldered most of the burden of raising a family. She had

Buy the Truth and Sell it Not

help from Jim's brother Joe, who lived in the house with the family and did much of the farm work, from plowing to killing hogs.64 Early on, he would provide the main male role model for the children. Gaston once told about watching while his Uncle Joe killed a snake in the barn that had been eating their eggs. The subject of eggs reminded him of a time when he was plowing, "When I was a lad down there on a small Franklin County farm, in the spring of the year I used to plough up lizard eggs along the side of the rail fences, and the mamma lizard (I suppose it was) would scurry over to hide under the fence."65

After chores were done, Gaston would find time for playing, as all boys do. He played baseball games with his friends. In his later years, it seemed to bring back pleasant memories to Gaston whenever he saw boys playing marbles. Of course, any boy who had a creek nearby would have a constant source of entertainment. Claude Hall, who preached all over Tennessee and became president of

Oklahoma Christian College, must have spent some time at Salem because he wrote to Gaston later about the pleasant hours they had spent at Beans Creek.66

Schooling was also part of his life. One photograph shows Gaston at Huntland Academy in a large group of students, including his two sisters. Gaston's first Bible class teacher was his great-aunt, Anne Elizabeth Hunt Moore, who taught a group of children at the schoolhouse in Huntland. We saw earlier that this same Annie Hunt Moore wrote an obituary in 1870 for her grandmother, Ann Day

Dear Hearts and Gentle People

Lipscomb. When Mrs. Moore died in 1932, Gaston helped perform the service. Gaston said she was "One of the three women who have influenced my life most...She taught us the evils of bad habits. While in her class I signed a pledge card promising to abstain from intoxicating liquors."[67]

Anne Elizabeth Hunt Moore

The search for truth was important to Gaston. Later, it would be the focus of a spiritual battle in his life. Learning truths at church or at school or on the farm were all ways to make a person better and help to avoid some of "de troubles of de world."

Buy the Truth and Sell it Not

Chapter 5
The Iron Horse

During the war, the railroad had brought trouble to the area in the form of Union soldiers. After the war, it brought commerce and growth. For Gaston Collins, it brought a world of opportunity. The railroad did for travel across the country what the airlines later did for world travel - made it accessible to everyone. If not for the railroad, many things would have been impossible for Gaston.

Dear Hearts and Gentle People

The first high school in Franklin County opened in the fall of 1906 in Decherd, using the facilities of the old Terrill College. Gaston Collins was there, fifteen years old and fifteen miles from home. The first year curriculum was Beginning Algebra, American Authors, Geology of Tennessee, and American Biography.[68]

Franklin County High School 1906

A train schedule from a few years later shows the train leaving Huntland at 7:02 a.m. and Beans Creek at 7:07 each day, with stops in Maxwell, Belvidere, and Winchester, before arriving in Decherd at 7:50 a.m. Gaston would usually step off the train at each station and talk with people on the platform until the train left.[69] His habit was to talk until the train began moving and then hop on at the last moment.[70]

Decherd Depot

It was a long day for Gaston. According to the train schedule, the only train leaving Decherd after noon departed at 6:45 p.m., arriving in Huntland at 7:23 p.m.

Buy the Truth and Sell it Not

Gaston wrote, "...I went on the train to school, catching the early morning train and returning on a late one after dark. I would take an oil lantern to the station of morning, so I could have it at night to guide me out home to the country when the nights were dark and the roads muddy. Those were the days when we didn't have a car, but I had no Daddy to have a car – he'd been called from earth long before that. I still have and cherish that old lantern; it's hanging in my garage...."[71]

A new school opened in Huntland in 1907. A picture from the time shows Gaston as a student there. Besides farm work during his high school years, Gaston may have provided money for his schooling by working at one of the local factories, such as the faucet factory in Beans Creek, which produced cedar faucets for barrels.[72] When Gaston graduated, his declamation was on "Truth, the Object of all Studies."[73]

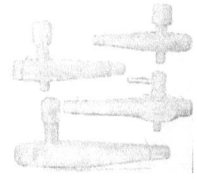

Cedar Faucets

One of Gaston's composition books from the time has essays about Abraham Lincoln, Paul Revere, a Washington vs. Philadelphia baseball game, a Missouri ghost story, a fight between two boys,

Dear Hearts and Gentle People

and a story of how a daughter helped her mother. One of his essays concerns a Huntland-Kelso baseball game and is entitled "My Last Railway Journey." It is reprinted in Appendix A. His composition book also contains some drawings he sketched.

Gaston's High School Sketches

In addition to beginning high school in 1906, Gaston also began his Christian life that same year, being baptized by James K. Hill. The following year, O.H. Tallman of Canada held a gospel meeting at Salem Church of Christ. Thirty people became Christians, including Gaston's sisters, Mollie and Willie.[74]

Canadian Red Ensign

Section II

O Canada!

Buy the Truth and Sell it Not

O.H. Tallman

O.E. Tallman

O Canada!

Chapter 6
The Remarkable Tallmans

The Restoration Movement which passed through Tennessee and created Salem Church of Christ had also passed through Canada. In Nova Scotia, a church was established in the town of River John in 1815. About 1832, a number of people separated from the Baptist Church in Hants County, Nova Scotia after refusing to swear to the *Articles of Faith and Practice* and to being led only by ordained clergy. These began meeting in small groups of the church of Christ in the towns of West Gore, Rawdon, Newport, Nine Mile River, and Shubenacadie.[75]

At the beginning of the twentieth century, some digression began to creep into these churches, with some people advocating organizational bodies outside the New Testament pattern, and some people advocating instrumental music. Members of the church in Nova Scotia who were concerned about these trends recruited a young preacher from Ontario who was a vibrant champion of restoration principles, O.H. Tallman.

Ora Hubert (O.H.) Tallman was born in 1876 in Smithville, Ontario. After deciding to give his life to preaching, he studied at Beamsville Bible School in Ontario, Carman Bible School in Manitoba, and Potter Bible College in Bowling Green, Kentucky. His younger brother Ozro Ellis (O.E.) Tallman, born in 1883, also studied at Carman Bible School and Potter Bible College. After both brothers graduated from the Bowling Green school, O.H. held a series of meetings throughout Tennessee, including the one at Old Salem when Gaston's two sisters were baptized.[76]

Buy the Truth and Sell it Not

Going to the West Gore, Nova Scotia congregation in 1908, O.H. had a good year there, (including a December 22 meeting in which they chopped a hole in the ice for a baptism![77]) O.H. Tallman and Donald McDougall conceived the idea of a Bible college in Nova Scotia to help evangelize the region. They also convinced younger brother O.E. to join them, and plans for Maritime Bible and Literary College were set into motion.

O.H. and O.E. Tallman were very much in the tradition of David Lipscomb and James A. Harding. They sought a middle path[78] between extremes of digressives who wanted extra-church societies and mechanical instruments of music on one side, and extreme conservatives on the other side, who wanted no Sunday schools, no located preachers, and no Bible colleges. The Maritime Bible and Literary College was to succeed for only a short time in this middle path.

Throughout their lives, O.H. and O.E. Tallman would preach throughout Canada and the United States. O.H. married Hallie Richardson, a girl from Richardsville, Kentucky. O.E. married a girl from West Gore, Nova Scotia, Mabel Wallace Covey, who was a cousin[79] of the girl Gaston would later marry. O.E. performed Gaston's wedding. Gaston would later preach at a congregation where another Tallman brother attended, and when Oliver Tallman, the Tallman's father passed away, Gaston helped perform the service.

O.E. passed from this life at age 47 in St. Catherines, Ontario, where he was living and preaching. O.H., who continued preaching as well as becoming a chiropractic doctor, died at age 79 in Pensacola, Florida. Speaking of O.H. Tallman, Gaston said, "If I am worth anything at all to the church, I owe considerable to Bro. Tallman for

O Canada!

suggesting and urging that I embark on my present career."[80]

**Maritime Bible and Literary College
West Gore, Nova Scotia**

Buy the Truth and Sell it Not

ANNOUNCEMENT

—OF THE—

Maritime Bible

=AND=

Literary College

WEST GORE
Hants Co., Nova Scotia, Canada

Announcements for 1909-1910

THE BIBLE STUDENT Press Print
Meaford, Ontario, Canada

O Canada!

Chapter 7
College Years

Maritime Bible and Literary College opened its doors for the first time on October 25, 1909 in the town of West Gore, Nova Scotia. Gaston Collins was there, eighteen years old and seventeen hundred miles from home. The college colors were blue and white, representing truth and purity, and the student body subscribed to those principles. One of the students, Loney MacDougall said, "There was a period when the college was running when the air was so pure you never heard a swear word; no tobacco or liquor sold; you had to go to Clarkesville to get them. An outsider going to the college said he thought he was spreading wings."[81]

Gaston's life at this point echoed his description of Abraham Lincoln in Gaston's high school composition book, "Lincoln came into the estate of manhood morally clean. He had formed no bad habits that would cause years of struggle to overcome. He had committed no deed that would bring the blush of shame to his cheeks. He was as free from vice as from crime. He was not profane; he had never tasted liquor; he was no brawler; he never gambled; he was honest and truthful."

Gaston Collins remained true to that quest for purity all his life. Years later, Gaston attended a public meeting where the speaker of the night continually used God's name in vain. After a bit, Gaston stood up in place and waited till the speaker paused and looked at him. Then Gaston said, "Sir, I cannot bear to hear the name of my Lord used in vain," and then he turned and walked out.[82] If Gaston went into a restaurant and discovered that it

Buy the Truth and Sell it Not

served alcohol, he would leave. After the invention of television, if Gaston was visiting someone who was watching television (he never owned one himself), when a beer commercial came on, he would get up and leave the room.[83]

That first year of school, Gaston was elected president of the class. The school year ended April 8, and Gaston preached that summer at Mill Village, Nova Scotia, just west of Shubenacadie and home to many of the Wallace family. The second year of college began October 17, 1910, and Gaston was elected president of the Philomathian Club, which means "lover of learning." The club had weekly meetings with readings, essays, orations, and vocal and instrumental music. A new teacher was added to the faculty that year, Miss Ada Simm, who taught Latin, Botany, and English Composition.

When he first came to college, Gaston boarded with Lorenzo and Ella Simm. They had supported the college and donated land to it. They had an extra boy's room in their home because their son Morris was away in Montreal working.[84] So it was natural that they would board one of the students.

They also had three daughters at home. Etha was three and a half years older than Gaston; Violetta was three and a half years younger, and Evelyn was another year younger than that. By the second year of school, the twenty year old southern gentlemen in their midst was drawing quite a bit of attention in the household, especially from the youngest, Evelyn. That was when the other sister, Ada, came home from Montreal, where she had been working, to begin teaching at the college.

O Canada!

Many, many years later there was a popular song entitled "Did You Ever Have to Make Up Your Mind?" about a young man who had to choose between two sisters. That is the situation Gaston apparently faced. Whether things were getting too complicated at the Simm household, or whether Gaston just got a good employment opportunity is unclear, but Gaston moved. By the time of the 1911 census in West Gore, he was living with Foster Brison, another one of the teachers at the school, and the owner of a shingle mill. It is also unclear whether Gaston stopped going to school temporarily, or whether he went to school and also worked at the shingle mill.[85] The 1911 census shows that he worked 40 weeks in1911, at an average of 60 hours per week, and earned $329 that year. Perhaps on top of that he also got free room and board.

Maple Leaf Quartet:
E. Gaston Collins, L.J. Keffer, Fred L. Wallace, and O.E. Tallman

Gaston wasn't completely disconnected from the school, or perhaps he came back during the school year, for the 1911-1912 school year was when the Maple Leaf Quartet began performing. It featured Gaston and L. J. Keffer as

Buy the Truth and Sell it Not

tenors, Fred Wallace as bass and O.E. Tallman as baritone. They performed eighteen concerts at various locations, advertising the school, and collecting sixty dollars for the temperance cause.[86] One of their concerts was in Windsor, about twenty-five miles southwest of the college. The *Windsor Tribune* reported, "The hall at St. Croix was filled with an attentive and delighted audience. The program consisted of solos, quartettes, readings, etc, and there wasn't one weak number during the whole entertainment."[87]

> Quartet –
> L. to R. –
> E. Gaston Collins, Tenor.
> L. J. Keffer, First Tenor.
> Fred L. Wallace, Bass.
> O. E. Tallman, Baritone.
> Maritime Bible & Literary College,
> West Gore, N.S.,
> Canada.
> 1910 to 1914.

Gaston's Caption on Quartet Picture

O Canada!

During the summer of 1912, Gaston preached in Franklin City, Kentucky, and also got to visit home and family for the first time in almost three years. The 1912-1913 school year saw Gaston back in school, participating in a musical workers class. He graduated at the end of the year with a degree of Bachelor of Expression, a three year degree designed for public speakers.

In the spring of 1913, *The Bible Student* reported that Gaston and Gordon McPhee would travel to Carman and Rosebank, Manitoba. Gaston was described by O.E. Tallman as "a splendid singer as well as a preacher of no mean ability."[88] McPhee's plans changed when a Nova Scotia church offered him employment, but Gaston continued with the Manitoba work that summer. The congregation at Carman had been established in 1889 and included many settlers who had come from Meaford, Ontario. The Tennessee preacher and educator James A. Harding had preached there, and McPhee would later preach there from 1917 to 1920. A Bible school had been established in Carman in 1899 and had been attended by both the Tallman brothers.

At the end of the summer, Gaston returned to the college in Nova Scotia to teach sight singing and mathematics. On Wednesday, October 22, 1913, he and Ada Simm were married, with O.E. Tallman performing the ceremony. They had a short honeymoon in Truro and Halifax, and Gaston returned to his teaching.

Buy the Truth and Sell it Not

O Canada!

Chapter 8
Ada

Ada Alberta Tupper Simm was born December 2, 1888 in the village of Rawdon Gold Mines, Hants County, Nova Scotia to Lorenzo Dow Simm and Ella Wallace Simm. Both of her parents' roots went deep into Scotland, with Wallace, especially being an old and honored name there. Ada used to tell the story of one of her ancestors who was the captain of the royal guard in Scotland and whose daughter ran away with a footman. (This story is heard so often in genealogical circles that some consider it apocryphal.) There was also a branch of her family tree outside of Scotland, including a *Mayflower* passenger, a Salem witch, and relatives of Benjamin Franklin.

Lorenzo Dow Simm

Ada's father had been named for the flamboyant backwoods preacher, Lorenzo Dow, and while her father was a shopkeeper rather than a preacher, he supported the work of the church, especially teaching the young. Ada's mother taught Sunday school, and evidently passed her love of teaching on to Ada. After completing her schooling, Ada obtained her teaching certificate at age sixteen. She taught for a few years before she came to Maritime Bible and Literary

Daddy Simm's Store

Buy the Truth and Sell it Not

College. Later on, when her family struggled financially, she would use her teaching skills to be the breadwinner.

Besides teaching, Ada apparently felt called to be a preacher's wife. Foster Brison, who employed Gaston in his shingle mill, had been so smitten with Ada that he built a house to woo her. Ada didn't want a house though; she wanted a preacher, and had briefly considered a Baptist preacher before Gaston landed on her doorstep.[89]

In Ada, it seems God found the perfect help-meet for Gaston. She was always willing to do whatever was necessary for the ministry. She would teach women in the congregation, send supplies to missionaries, take care of Gaston and the children, and make wherever they were living at the time a welcoming, well-run home.

Mr. and Mrs. Gaston Collins

In their wedding photo, we see Ada as a tall, slender figure, about 5'5" tall, with an oval face and fair complexion, blue to hazel eyes, and long straight brown hair that she wore up on her head.[90] Except for a little different hairstyle, this is the way she looked all her life.

Gaston, just slightly shorter than Ada, would be described as medium height and medium build, with blue eyes and wavy, auburn hair.[91] The tenor voice and red hair likely

O Canada!

came from his mother's Irish genes.[92] As he aged, his auburn hair turned first a gunmetal grey and then white.[93] If Gaston was ever self-conscious about being slightly younger and slightly shorter than his wife, he never gave an indication of it, except perhaps in the wedding photo, where he is standing on a higher step to bring him above Ada's level.

Ada was perhaps the first amateur photographer in the family, as several photographs of Gaston from the time were likely taken by her. One picture was possibly taken on their honeymoon. Gaston is seated in front of a falls, possibly Waddell Falls of Victoria Park in Truro, Nova Scotia.[94] Another photograph of Gaston was probably taken shortly after their marriage. It shows him traipsing through the snow in his boots, carrying two buckets of water. It is captioned "1st house + original water system." Gaston doesn't appear to mind carrying water for his new bride, but seems to be happy and full of enthusiasm for life and for the work of the church. Little did he know, however, that he was about to be blindsided by a spiritual storm headed straight for his world.

Buy the Truth and Sell it Not

West Gore Church Building

Chapter 9
The Attack

Daniel Sommer and his son Fred were complex figures in church history. Deeply committed to the Restoration Movement, they had strong opinions and freely expressed them. As the movement struggled with the questions of missionary societies and instrumental music, Daniel strongly opposed both. In 1889, 5000 church leaders gathered at Sand Creek, Illinois to consider these questions. It was the Sand Creek Declaration, of which Daniel Sommer had a part, which largely closed the door in many people's minds to any hope of fellowship between

O Canada!

instrumental and acappella churches. Speaking of instrumental churches, it said, "We cannot and we will not regard them as brethren."[95]

Sommer was not opposed to all innovations. He had no problem with Sunday schools, which some opposed, or multiple communion cups, which others opposed. He was very opposed, however, to educated preachers. The Restoration Movement set forth the priesthood of all believers, and that all should teach and exhort one another. Going beyond this, Sommer said, would lead to preacher cults and the "high sounding oratory of collegiate men"[96] leading people astray.

Sommer is correct that such things can happen, but he incorrectly identified the problem as the education, instead of the heart of the man. A study of scripture shows that education is completely in line with God's will. Indeed, some would say that general education cannot be separated from religious education, because "All truth is God's truth."[97] The scribes and the Pharisees were not condemned for their education, but for how they used it. Or as Mark Twin succinctly put it, "Education makes a good man better and a bad man worse."

In his later years, Sommer became more tolerant of the opinions of others. He attended the National Unity meeting in Indianapolis in 1939 seeking ways to reunite the branches of the Restoration Movement.[98] He spoke at some of the Bible colleges which he had opposed. His later positions, though, had little of the impact of those from his younger days.

Daniel Sommer's oldest son Fred was very much in the same mold as his father. He said Bible colleges "are uncalled for, as they accomplish nothing that could not be better done in another and better way."99 Before the opening of Maritime Bible and Literary College, Fred Sommer had preached in the West Gore Church of Christ. After O.H. Tallman left the West Gore congregation for health reasons, Sommer returned in 1914, and it wasn't long before a division in the congregation occurred. Students and staff of the college and their supporters began holding church services at the college.

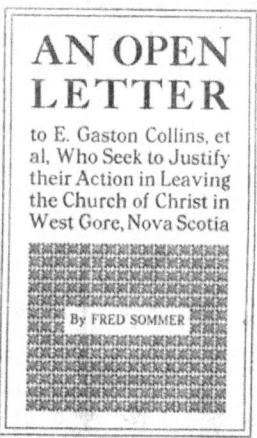

After the split, Fred Sommer produced a sixteen page tract entitled "AN OPEN LETTER to E. Gaston Collins, et al, Who Seek to Justify their Action in Leaving the Church of Christ in West Gore, Nova Scotia." In one of his statements directed at Collins, he sometimes referred to himself in the third person. "You have proclaimed far and wide, that the asking of a 'digressive' preacher to preach in this church was the wedge that split the church. I deny this, totally. Said preacher had often preached here before. He labored for the congregation once for a year. His ministry was acceptable, and he is held in high esteem yet by the people. He was not wishing or asking to preach. The people simply wished him to."100

This split in the West Gore congregation did not result in the congregation becoming more conservative, but more digressive, as Gaston had claimed. Within a few years the church had begun accepting more innovations, such as instrumental music in worship. Despite the words between them, Gaston never seemed to consider Fred

O Canada!

Sommer as his enemy. In the 1950's, Gaston and Ada were still exchanging Christmas cards with Mrs. Fred Sommer.

As if the local church split and the health of Brother Tallman weren't enough blows to the college, the year 1914 dealt it another blow. On August 4, Britain declared war on Germany. Most Canadians still considered themselves a part of the British Empire. Canada had become an independent confederation in 1867, but Canadians still flew either the flag of Great Britain, the Union Jack (the Royal Union Flag), or the Canadian Red Ensign, which had the Union Jack in one corner. The day after Britain declared war on Germany, Canada also declared war. Young men who might have thought of going to college began immediately signing up to go to war. College continued through the spring of 1915, and after that, was suspended indefinitely.

James Wallace, Gaston Collins,
Esther Wallace, Ella Simm,
Ada Collins, Claire Collins

There was one bright spot in 1914 for Gaston and Ada Collins. On September 22, their first child, Elizabeth Claire, was born. On the birth certificate, Gaston's first name is given as Edward instead of Edwin (a mistake that would be repeated on his Social Security card). Gaston's occupation is listed as Evangelist.

Evangeline Postage Stamp

Section III

The Evangelist

Buy the Truth and Sell it Not

Chapter 10
Survival

Henry Wadsworth Longfellow's epic poem *Evangeline* tells the story of the Acadian people forced out of Canada and New England, primarily because of their religion. Many of them sought refuge in the American South, in Louisiana in particular, where the name Acadian was shortened to Cajun. The name Evangeline means bearer of good tidings, the same root word from which we get evangelist, a bearer of the gospel.

Gaston Collins, the evangelist, was in his own way forced out of Canada. The college where he had begun teaching closed down. With a new wife and baby, he needed some means of support. His old job at the shingle mill may not have been available, since the owner had also lost his teaching job. More importantly, the thing Gaston most wanted to be, an evangelist, was going to be difficult in a place where the church was divided and struggling.

One of Gaston's classmates at the college and fellow Tennessean, Mr. Orange Lemon Northcut of Warren County, Tennessee, found employment in Nova Scotia by joining the army. On June 22, 1918, he joined the Royal Canadian Engineers Overseas Expeditionary Force. It's not known if he made it overseas before the end of the war. He did eventually return to Grundy County, Tennessee where he lived out his years. For Gaston Collins, however, raised in David Lipscomb's teachings of remaining separate from civil government, the army would not have been an option, even if he had been single.

Like Evangeline, Gaston also sought refuge in the South, going home to Tennessee. Maritime Bible and Literary

The Evangelist

College closed in the spring of 1915. That summer, Gaston enrolled in State Teachers College in Murfreesboro, Tennessee where he reviewed three classes (similar to auditing a class).[101] The classes which he took, Biology, English, and History, were possibly preparing him to take a teachers examination so he could teach public school.

Just up the road in Nashville, an event took place in 1915 that was to have an impact on Gaston's life many years later. R.H. Boll was forced to resign his position as editor of the *Gospel Advocate* magazine because of theological disagreements he had with the owner. A more immediate impact on Gaston's life would have been realized sometime that summer - Ada was expecting again.

After finishing his classes in Murfreesboro, Gaston either returned to Nova Scotia to escort his wife, or perhaps sent for her to come with the baby. In October 1915, Ada made her first trip to Tennessee, traveling by train through New Brunswick, Quebec, and Ontario before passing Niagara Falls on the way south.[102] It's not clear whether this roundabout trip was dictated by war restrictions,[103] or whether it was simply a chance to sightsee.

The young family was now living in Huntland, Tennessee, where Gaston's mother, Lizzie Collins, lived. Lizzie was affectionately known to her children and grandchildren as Mamie (pronounced `măm ē). The year 1916 brought both death and life to the family. Mamie's father, J.B. O'Neal, died January 12, 1916.[104] On February 9, the "middle child" Verna Mae was born to Gaston and Ada.

J.B. O'Neal

Buy the Truth and Sell it Not

It's unclear exactly what Gaston was doing during this year. Taking teachers examinations, trying to find a congregation that needed a preacher, helping family members, working at the local faucet factory,[105] or living off his mother's kindness are all possibilities. Perhaps all of these were happening at once. If Gaston was working at the faucet factory, the irony was probably not lost on him of a preacher producing items that among other uses, helped people to tap beer kegs.

Ada had a stressful time. Raising two babies, perhaps living with her mother-in-law, and trying to get by on little or no income while far away from all former family and friends had to be hard on her. One time, while picking apples for the family, she began crying, no doubt homesick for the beautiful apple orchards of Nova Scotia, and her family and friends there.[106]

November of 1916 brought the presidential election, with the candidate winning who promised to keep America out of the war. January of 1917 brought the Zimmerman telegrams, with Mexico threatening to go to war against America. On April 6, America entered the war. War meant registering for the draft, and Gaston, who normally avoided civil government, obeyed the law and registered.

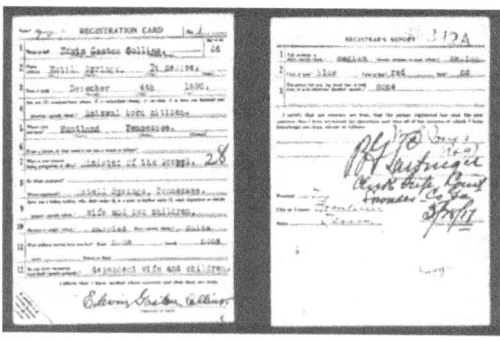

The Evangelist

His draft card, dated May 28, 1917 lists his home address as Estill Springs, Tennessee and his occupation as minister of the gospel. He claimed exemption from the draft because of a dependent wife and children. The family also lived for awhile with Gaston's mother Mamie in Decherd.

In the fall of 1917 the family boarded the train and moved to St. Elmo, near Lookout Mountain in the Chattanooga, Tennessee area.[107] It was probably at this time that Gaston preached for a church in LaFayette, Georgia, just south of Chattanooga.

In May of 1918, Ada took Claire and Verna on the train for the first visit home in almost three years. Daddy Simm, Ada's father, no doubt paid for her trip so he could see his daughter and grandchildren. Gaston stayed behind to preach. This time, Ada took the train to New York and evidently felt safe enough to take a boat to Boston.

Verna and Claire's passport photo

From Boston on to Nova Scotia, however, they took the train to avoid any submarines.[108] Once again, during the summer, while Ada was in Canada and Gaston in the South, they discovered that Ada was expecting.

55

Buy the Truth and Sell it Not

On July 1, 1918, Gaston received his certificate to teach second grade in Tennessee[109], but it doesn't seem he ever used it. That summer Gaston held a meeting at the church in Trenton, Alabama, east of Huntsville. Ada and the girls returned south in August, and that fall the family moved to Huntsville, Alabama.[110]

In Huntsville, they lived near the streetcar line, and the girls learned from their cousin Collins Steensland the trick of putting straight pins on the track in certain shapes to have them pressed into a permanent design by the streetcar. One Sunday morning the girls were dressed for church and told to go outside and play without getting dirty. A little later they were found making mud pies and when asked where they got the water for the mud, Verna said, "I peed on it." Once, Ada left them alone for a little bit and for some reason, told them not to put beans up their noses while she was gone. When she returned, Claire had succumbed to the power of suggestion and had a bean up her nose which the doctor had to remove.

More and more young men were being drafted for the war, and Ada was fearful that Gaston would be next. Finally, news came that the Armistice was signed on November 11, and there were great celebrations and ringing of bells. Ada was relieved that she would not be left alone with the children while Gaston went off to war.

Joy was short-lived, however. The great H1N1 flu epidemic, which had begun that summer and would

The Evangelist

eventually kill five percent of the world's population, struck Gaston and Ada. Verna remembers that she and Claire were sick in bed together and that a neighbor girl brought them violets. They were all so sick that Mamie came to take care of everyone. The symptoms of the flu included joint and muscle pain, often treated with oils and spices. Verna remembers Gaston sitting backwards in a chair in front of the fire, while Ada rubbed his back. On February 5, 1919, the third daughter, Wilma Glenn was born. Whether this was before or after Ada had the flu is not clear. Thankfully, everyone survived the flu.

Dallas Church of Christ, Huntsville, AL

Gaston would later list his first regular preaching assignment as beginning in 1920 in Algood,[111] but indications are that he did quite a bit in 1919 in Huntsville, Alabama. A newspaper note from October 5 shows him preaching at the Dallas Church of Christ in Huntsville. One from November 12 shows him performing a wedding.[112] The following February he wrote an obituary for the *Gospel Advocate* for a Huntsville mother who died of flu complications.[113]

The hard times weren't over, but things were beginning to get better. The young family had survived spiritual attack, unemployment, major disruptions, major moves, three pregnancies, and the killer flu. Now they were ready to begin greater service to God.

Buy the Truth and Sell it Not

Chapter 11
Algood, Lipscomb and Bridgeport

In December of 1920, Gaston turned thirty years old. Just before that, according to him, he had his first regular preaching duties in Algood and Livingston, Tennessee. We have a picture of the house in which they lived. We know that Claire, six years old in 1920, started school there.[114] We know that Verna, who turned five years old in 1921, started school there at age five. According to her, she started school early

The Evangelist

because she could already read and because she was too much of a handful for Mamie.[115] Mamie, at some point, came to live with them, to take care of the baby, Wilma, while Ada taught. We know that in October 1922, Ada had a contract with the Putnam County Board of Education to teach at Algood. Whether or not she taught in Algood before then is unknown.

> The Brief History of the Algood Church of Christ says: "In 1900 William Henry Goolsby, Mrs. John Epperson, Grant Cox, and Mrs. Robert A. Cox met on Sunday afternoons to conduct worship services in a building called Greenwood building. The men would lead in prayer, read from the Bible, and all would sing and observe the Lord's Supper. Later Brother E.G. Collins came from Nashville one Sunday each month to preach for the noon and evening services; he stayed in the home of Mrs. John McCormick. Mrs. Will Swallows prepared the Lord's Supper for the worship services. The church grew and in 1917 a building was erected at the corner of Qualls and Wall streets."

It is difficult to mesh this history exactly with the facts we know about Gaston's life, except that Gaston was apparently the first preacher at Algood Church of Christ, and that he also at some point came one Sunday each month.

To supplement the preacher's salary, the church would sometimes give the family a "pounding."[116] Someone would give them a pound of flour, someone else a pound of sugar, someone else a dressed chicken, etc., etc. (Note: there are probably preachers today who need a pounding, but it's of a different type, and for a different reason – to knock some sense into them!)

Buy the Truth and Sell it Not

The first Christmas Verna remembers was in Algood. One of the church members made the girls a stuffed cloth farmer boy in overalls, and a stuffed cloth rabbit in a checkered outfit. Ada baked cakes and cookies. They put strings of popcorn and looped paper chains on the tree. Gaston lit the candles on the tree. When electric tree lights first became available, Gaston didn't want to use them because, like many people of the time, he considered electric lights to be more dangerous than candles!

In 1922, Gaston led the singing at a twelve day meeting at Old Salem church in Huntland. The article by H.R. Moore in the October 12, 1922 *Gospel Advocate* said:

> "A.B. Lipscomb did the preaching. E. Gaston Collins of Algood led the singing.... Lipscomb and Collins are of pioneer ancestors. Each and his father were born near Salem....Each is highly respected by mutual friends and relatives in the Old Salem and adjacent localities. Their equipments for usefulness are of the best. Lipscomb is cultured and has a clear conception of the subject matter he proposes to present and is successful in imparting it to others. Collins is similarly endowed and gifted. Each is fortunately mated to a superior manager."[117]

Also in 1922, Gaston decided to enter David Lipscomb College. Ada's teaching position with the Algood school and Mamie's willingness to be live-in babysitter made this possible. In spite of the troubles she had seen in life, Mamie was apparently always happy and full of fun and jokes. Once she dressed herself and Wilma in old clothes and convinced the neighbors that they were beggars. Mamie loved to tell the story about being on the train with her three granddaughters when a stranger sized them up and, pointing to Claire said, "That's the pretty one," then

The Evangelist

to Wilma, "That's the cute one," and finally to Verna, "That's the mean one."

Mamie
Mary Elizabeth (Lizzie) O'Neal Collins

Buy the Truth and Sell it Not

Greek Club, Gaston on left

Gaston lived on campus at Lipscomb during the week and came home by train at least some weekends to preach and see his family. Possibly this was when he preached one Sunday each month at the Algood church. He took a class in Greek, a class in church history, and two Bible classes. The 1923 yearbook *The Backlog* shows him in the Tennessee club, the Greek club, the Glee club, the Preachers club, and the Literary society. He received the most votes (40 out of 88) in a class vote for best preacher.

Preachers Club

The Evangelist

THE SCHOOL QUARTETTE

Robert M. Williams
E. Gaston Collins
David F. Bryant
M. Clarke Mercer

He was also in the school quartette, one of the editors of a school paper *The Havalind Acts,* and a member of the debate team. He participated in a three-way debate with Harper Christian College and Abilene Christian College. The topic of the debate was "Resolved, that the United States should join the League of Nations." Gaston debated in the affirmative at home and denied it at Harper.[118] Debating both sides of an issue helps a person to better understand the opinions of those who oppose you. Gaston would have need of this skill later in life.

Buy the Truth and Sell it Not

Gaston did not complete the school year at Lipscomb. His grades for fall and winter quarters averaged 95 in each Bible class, 94 in Greek, and 87 in church history. His transcript says he dropped out in May.[119] He was moving the family from Algood, Tennessee to Bridgeport, Alabama, where he would preach from 1923 to 1925.

Bridgeport Church Building

Bridgeport, east of Huntsville, was described by Claire as such:

> "It is situated at a bend of the Tennessee River and the scenery is very pretty. The main part of town is situated some distance from the river and we used to visit a girl friend who lived in a very pretty place near the river. We always 'dressed up' in fancy clothes when we went there and had a wonderful time pretending we were 'somebody.' Then we would just be ourselves and sit on the stone fence that surrounded the yard, and eat peaches from the peach orchard. We spent about a month in the summer on Cumberland Mountain about three miles from Bridgeport. There were about twenty little cottages at this place, and in front of them was 'The Bluff,' a large flat rock projecting out from the mountain. Here we had picnics and made bonfires at night and toasted marshmallows. The scenery from the bluff was beautiful. You could see for miles and miles and the Tennessee River looked like a tiny stream winding along the valley. A little distance behind the cottages were springs of sulphur and iron water, and many people spent the summer here for the benefit of the water."[120]

The Evangelist

In 1924, the second summer in Bridgeport, Gaston and Ada took the girls to Nova Scotia, traveling by train to Norfolk, Virginia, boat to Boston, another boat to Yarmouth, Nova Scotia, and then the train to West Gore. A photograph from the time shows Gaston and the girls visiting the public gardens of Halifax, Nova Scotia.  The family would get together at the home of Ada's parents in West Gore. Ada's sister Evelyn, the best pianist in the family, would play the piano and everyone would sing.

Public Gardens of Halifax, N.S.

At the end of the summer, Gaston, Ada and the girls took the boat to Boston, and then the train through New York, Washington and Chattanooga to home.

Gaston at the dock

In Bridgeport, the family lived first with the Ed Lloyd family in their large home, then in an apartment above a bank, and finally, in a preacher's house that the congregation acquired. While

Buy the Truth and Sell it Not

Gaston with Sara Nell Lloyd

in Bridgeport, the family bought an upright piano for the girls and Ada to play. This piano would travel with them through many moves.[121] In 1924, Gaston began a habit that he would continue for many, many years. He began on January 1 reading the Bible, and in the course of the year, read it completely through.

Also in 1924, there was a news item which proclaimed, "We have received a splendid little book (24 pages) entitled *Unequal Yoking* written by E. Gaston Collins, Bridgeport, Ala. It is described as 'a treatise on the Christian's relationship to the world.' Obtainable from the author, or through this office, at 10 cents each, $1 per dozen."[122] Gaston wrote *Unequal Yoking*[123] because he believed that God calls Christians to have a much greater separation from worldly organizations than many Christians envision. Whether you agree with his study or not, it is good for Christians to examine themselves on this subject and not just blindly follow what everyone else does. *Unequal Yoking* is reprinted in Appendix C.

It may be somewhat jarring to modern readers to realize that in 1923 there were people who believed you could be a Christian and a member of the Ku Klux Klan. The *Christian Leader* in 1923 had letters from people in Ohio and Indiana claiming that the Klan had wide popular

The Evangelist

support in their states and wanting to know if a Christian could be a member of that organization. Gaston responded with an eight point letter saying that membership in that kind of organization is contrary to God's word, regardless of what the organization practiced.[124] This letter was incorporated into *Unequal Yoking* the next year.

Unequal Yoking

OR

"Be Not Unequally Yoked With Unbelievers."

"What Does It Mean?"

Being a treatise on the relationship of the Christian to the world.

By
E. GASTON COLLINS.

Buy the Truth and Sell it Not

Meaford Church of Christ, 1920s

Meaford Church of Christ building, 2013

The Evangelist

Chapter 12
Meaford by the Bay

In 1925 Gaston moved the family to Meaford, Ontario, located at the south end of Georgian Bay, a large arm of Lake Huron. Gaston's friends the Tallmans were from this area, and their brother Shep Tallman lived in Meaford. Gordon McPhee, Gaston's friend from college had also preached here. It's these connections that likely brought Gaston north. Ada surely was pleased to be returning to her homeland, even if it was a different province. Border crossing records for May 13, 1925 show Gaston Collins and family crossing the border at Bridgeburg, Canada, just across from Buffalo, New York, headed for Meaford, Ontario.[125]

When Gaston first came up to try out at the Meaford Church of Christ, he stayed with the family of John Jay. On Sunday morning, he and Mrs. Jay entered the church building. No one else was in the vestibule. The doors to the auditorium were closed, and the church was as silent as a tomb. "No one's here!" Gaston said, and then discovered that the auditorium was full, with everyone sitting quietly waiting to begin worship. This was very different from the South, where people noisily talked and visited right up to time for service. Another culture shock had occurred at breakfast, when the Jays had made biscuits in honor of their southern guest. When Gaston asked where the biscuits were, he was told, "They're out in

Buy the Truth and Sell it Not

the snow, cooling." Gaston quickly retrieved them and told his hosts that southerners like their biscuits hot![126]

As the family was preparing to move, Ada warned her girls that when they reached Canada, they must not say "I done this," or "I done that," but use proper grammar. On the trip up, after they had gotten on the final leg of the train bound for Meaford, Gaston used the trip to sit down wherever there was an empty seat, introduce himself, and talk about Meaford. In this way, he already knew a lot of the people of the town when he arrived.

The family loved the preacher's house in Meaford. For one thing, it was the first indoor toilet they had ever had! It also had a beautiful balcony above the porch where the girls loved to sleep on summer nights. The house became the setting for lots of weddings performed by Gaston. Ada served cake and grape juice, and the girls would be the audience, to the point that they knew the ceremony by heart, "Dearly beloved, we are gathered here to join this man and woman in holy matrimony...."

Meaford House 2013

Ada had a wicker rocking chair with a swing-out basket underneath that she used for sewing. While in Meaford, Gaston bought a mantel clock that chimed the

The Evangelist

hours. Like their other furniture, this chair and clock traveled with them through many, many moves.[127]

Gaston stayed busy with preaching the gospel and ministering to the needs of the congregation. He organized a Friday night singing class. He was sometimes disdainful of people who spent their time in idle activities, such as at the bowling green, but he did find time for playing a little golf.[128] The girls enjoyed the recreational pursuits of the area,  swimming and picnicking in the summer, and skating and sledding in the winter.

To supplement the preacher's income, members of the congregation would give the family gallons of buttermilk and barrels of Northern Spy, Russet and other varieties of apples. Everyone had to be good stewards and not waste food. Once after Sunday service, Ada invited one of the sisters of the congregation home for dinner with them. "No thank you," she replied, "I have a little cheese that needs to be eaten."

Wherever Gaston went as an evangelist, he had a home church where he spent most of his time, but he also made regular visits to other churches nearby that didn't have a regular preacher or were in need of encouragement. Gaston never showed much interest in building up the

Buy the Truth and Sell it Not

body life of one congregation, or in building up his own body of sermons for deeper studies. His passion was for sowing the seed and spreading the good news of the gospel to as many places and as many people as he could. For this reason, every year or two he would submit his resignation to the elders of the congregation, to be re-hired or let go at their discretion. If he was not being effective where he was, he wanted to go spread the gospel elsewhere.

Gaston spent two weeks in March 1927 at Selkirk, Ontario on a peace mission. He reported, "The distressing division that has existed among the brethren at Selkirk for some years has been done away and the brethren are now meeting together. They worshipped together on Lord's days and also attended well the nightly meetings held during the week. The old officers resigned and new ones were selected. A good spirit prevailed and all enjoyed getting together. They had been praying for unity, and a number of confessions were made. A good work could be done in Selkirk, and I pray that it shall be done."[129]

In the summer of 1927, he visited small churches throughout Manitoulin Island (the largest freshwater island in the world, located in Lake Huron). He eventually ended up in Thessalon, Ontario, near Sault Ste. Marie, where he held a fifteen day meeting. He had some health problems that summer, reporting that he had lost forty pounds due to gallstones.[130] Stomach problems remained with him throughout life. Gaston could have found justification to use alcohol in the Apostle Paul's advice to "use a little wine for your stomachs sake." Instead, Gaston always used buttermilk or a little Dr. Pepper to ease his stomach.

Ada's father in Nova Scotia was suffering from atherosclerosis or hardening of the arteries. Once again,

The Evangelist

Gaston's dear mother Mamie came to the rescue, coming to Canada to take care of the girls while Ada visited her father. Mamie sometimes teased the girls about the "boogeyman," and Verna would always run past the attic door because she believed that was where the boogeyman must live. In 1928, Gaston added his name to a document signed by fourteen other brethren supporting his college friend, L.J. Keffer, whose second marriage was being called into question by some brethren.[131]

A missionary from Japan, Otoshige Fujimori, stayed with Gaston and Ada for awhile, and gave Ada a beautiful silk scarf or throw.[132] In April of 1928, the family took an Easter break to nearby St. Catherines, Ontario, where they visited their old friends, the O.E. Tallman family. They did a lot of sightseeing at Niagara Falls and other places,[133] and visited churches at Jordan, Beamsville, Hamilton, and Selkirk. In May of 1928, Ada's father, Lorenzo Dow Simm died. In the summer of 1928, Gaston revisited some of the churches he had visited the previous summer. In August, Gaston helped perform the service when the Tallman's father, Oliver passed away.

Mamie, Oto, & Ada

Buy the Truth and Sell it Not

CHRISTIAN MONTHLY REVIEW

Vol. XII   DECEMBER, 1927   No. 12

I know of nothing good that may not be perverted. The gift season of the year is near. Though it may be made base the spirit of giving is noble. Though our *Christmas* time may not be correct, and though there may be much in it objectionable; yet it is a glorious fact that Christ was born, and it is good to remember that the angels said, *Be not afraid; for behold, I bring you good tidings of great joy which shall be to all the people; for there is born to you this day in the city of David a Saviour, who is Christ the Lord.* . . . . .

*Glory to God in the highest,
And on earth peace among men
in whom he is well pleased.*

Give and receive in the Christ spirit, don't exchange. This is prompted by appreciation and thanksgiving. To properly give or receive cultivates gracefulness and charm. It makes us think of Him from whom cometh "every good and perfect gift." It calls to mind the greatest Gift —he who was *wounded for our transgressions, bruised for our iniquities, by whose stripes we are healed.* It will lead us to give our best to him, and cause us to keep faith with him. It has been said: "He is best prepared to face the New Year who has kept faith with the Old." *And without faith it is impossible to be well-pleasing unto him.*—E.G.C.

IN THIS ISSUE

Editorials	2	Our Exchanges	10
The Greatest Prayer, and the Blessed in Pray—E. C. S. Heman and Divine Contrasted—H. M. R. "No Limit to Error."—E. G. C.		News and Correspondence	12
		Encouragement	15
Missions	7	Church Directory	16

Printed in Chatham, Ont., by The Planet Ptg. House, for the Publishers of Christian Monthly Review, Meaford, Ontario.

The Evangelist

Chapter 13
The Editor

After Gaston had been in Meaford for a year, he became the editor of the *Christian Monthly Review*, a paper which had previously been published in West Gore, Nova Scotia. Donald McDougall, whom Gaston had known in West Gore, introduced Gaston to the readership. The introduction was given and received in good humor, but has a little bit of ribbing for the foreigner in their midst:

> "E. Gaston Collins, a native of the jungles of Tennessee, but a kinsman of the great David Lipscomb, a Bluenose by education, and now matrimonally, residentially, and occupationally, a Canadian. He will be all right, er – if the bishops will look after him a little, and – er, keep him under, in his place, doing his own work while they do theirs."

To which Gaston added, "So mote it be. – E.G.C."[134] (The word Bluenose in his introduction is the nickname for someone from Nova Scotia.)

Now, in addition to the subject of worldliness, which he had addressed in his *Unequal Yoking* paper, he would have the opportunity to write about many topics. On the subject of living, he wrote, "Life has been called a battlefield. It is also an opportunity – not to get or be served, but to serve and spend and be spent. It is an education. There are many things we must learn – many graces to add. It is a training. One should as he grows older become kind instead of crabbed; gentle and more considerate of others rather than harsh and indifferent."[135]

Buy the Truth and Sell it Not

Of those who minimize the importance of baptism, or say it's not essential to salvation, he wrote "It seems strange that the only thing that is really a test of the sinner's faith, and only an act of faith, the majority refuse to do. Baptism is not connected with salvation, only by faith. How can one be 'saved by faith' and refuse to do the first act of faith he is asked to do?"[136]

On action, he wrote, "There are times when we need power and zeal to DO, as much as, if not more than, we need to know WHAT to do. The apostles knew what to do, but were told to wait in Jerusalem till they were indued with power from on high, which, said Christ, would come when the Holy Spirit came upon them. So we need to be clothed with the Spirit of zeal, willingness, sincerity, devotion and sacrifice."[137]

On a reformation in Tolstoi's life, "He quit measuring life by what others did for him, and began measuring it by what he could do for others. Life is not measured by our accumulations, nor by our being served by others, but by what we contribute to the sum of human happiness. This is verified by the Saviour, 'But he that is greatest among you shall be your servant.' Matt. 23:11."[138]

On those "who have no place on their program for the precepts and ideals of the Bible. Some go further and read it to doubt and scorn it and oppose it. They accept willingly all the blessings to be derived from its influence in the world, yet are so destitute of gratitude they won't help propagate its principles, nor thank God for giving us such a book. Some say it is nothing but fables. Some say the Genesis account of the creation is untrue and childish. Others say the whale never swallowed Jonah. Still others say the virgin birth is a fable or a myth of the gods. In fact, where has not the sacred volume been attacked? It seems

The Evangelist

to me we should accept it at all points. Another has well said, "Cut the Scriptures anywhere and they bleed with the blood of the Lamb of God."[139]

On the modern day defilement of marriage with infidelity, "'For from within, out of the heart of men, evil thoughts proceed, fornication, thefts, murders, adulteries, covetings, wickedness, deceit, lasciviousness, an evileye, railing, pride, foolishness: all these things proceed from within, and defile the man.'...The marriage of one man to one woman is fundamental, and gives stability to society by making better homes. And *any one who strikes at the foundation of our home-life is a traitor to the best interests of the human family.*"[140]

On revival, "Without a vision people perish. We must make a full surrender of our lives. We have dwelt long and loud on baptism but is it not possible that we have neglected the birth of the Spirit, 'Ye must be born of water and of the Spirit.' 'If any man hath not the spirit of Christ, he is none of His.' We need not water-born members but water-born and spirit-born members. Our membership should be built up of members who are *godly,* in pulpit and pew, office and classroom, factory and workshop, church and home, and until then we will have no revival."[141]

On congregations working together, "There are dangers attending co-operation, and there are dangers in not co-operating. In co-operating we must guard against a loss of congregational independence, and a centralizing of power and influence. In not co-operating there is the danger that we become too individualistic, too exclusive, too much interested in self, which results in narrowness. Of course the way is *strait* and *narrow,* but the *field* of *operation* is the *world.* Neither a certain, loose broadmindedness, nor

Buy the Truth and Sell it Not

that deadening, blighting, vise-like narrowness are conducive to the growth of the church."[142]

On whether preachers should perform weddings for non-Christians, "While I do not wish to 'encourage in any way' improper marriage, yet I have officiated at the marriage of Christians to unbelievers, for my observation has been that to refuse to officiate is to make it many fold harder to approach the unbelieving one regarding his salvation. To refuse does not stop the marriage nor convert the unbeliever."[143]

One of Gaston's last, and happiest entries in the *Christian Monthly Review* came on page 8 of the October 1929 issue, "On Sept. 1, I was at Griersville in the morning and at Meaford again at night, at which time it was my happy privilege to take the confession of our two oldest daughters and baptise them the same hour of the night. At the same time their friend, Helen Whitfield, also obeyed the gospel, it being her 13th birthday."

Gaston, Verna, Claire, Wilma, Ada

The Evangelist

Chapter 14
The Father

Gaston's lack of a father during much of his childhood may have affected his own parenting abilities. His daughter believed he teased too much.[144] Teasing can be a learned behavior, and much of his teasing may have been learned from Mamie. Gaston teased his cat by putting paper boots on its feet, then laughing as it took each step and tried to shake off each boot. No permanent harm was done to the cat. He might drop a cat from head high to watch it land on its feet, or put it in a paper bag and watch it try to get out. He liked cats, though. The family frequently had a pet cat, including a solid black one he whimsically named Snowball. One acquaintance remembers him being very fond of his cat.[145]

His teasing sometimes extended to his children. If he was using a pocketknife to clean his fingernails, and one of the girls walked by, he might pretend to stab at her head with the knife, while having the blade covered by his thumb so it could do no harm. Psychologists say teasing can be compensation for feelings of inadequacy. Perhaps Gaston did not always know how to relate to his girls as a father, and teasing was a way of relating on some level.

Like many parents at the time, he had strict rules for his children. When his children were young, he would dish out their food, and they could not leave the table until they had cleaned their plates. Once when Wilma asked to get down from her high chair, Gaston instructed her to say please first. For some reason she would not say it, and he would not remove her from her chair. After Wilma fell

Buy the Truth and Sell it Not

asleep in the high chair, Ada finally convinced Gaston to take Wilma out and put her to bed.

Gaston could be a perfectionist. When the children took a bath, the tub had to be drained properly so as not to leave a ring. If they read the newspaper, he expected it to be folded back just like it had come from the rack. He liked to drive 45 to 50 miles per hour, which was fast for that time, and Ada would frequently ask, "Do you have to go so fast?" He hated waiting on others, and would frequently drive fast to arrive at appointments in the nick of time. This did not carry over to his church life, however, as he always arrived early to fellowship with others.

Neither did his perfectionism lead him to teach his daughters to be judgmental of others, as he usually was of a forgiving attitude that allowed for the frailties and opinions of others.

Gaston and Ada never gave the girls lots of praise, for fear of making them conceited. Other children might stand and recite poetry in front of a group, but the preacher's daughters were not allowed to draw attention to themselves in this way. They were occasionally allowed to play the piano for others, once performing a recital with a trio of all three sisters.[146]

Gaston and Ada did not give an abundance of physical affection to their girls. This was a time when many parents

The Evangelist

showed their love for their children by providing for them and training them properly, not by making them feel good about themselves. The girls were expected to be seen and not heard. It was a very reserved household.

Gaston and Ada trained their daughters to become Christian wives and mothers. When Verna later chose a career first, Gaston was dismissive of it. He called it her "little job."

Gaston was committed to the great commissions call to preach the gospel wherever it led him. He tried to minimize the impact on his family, but it was still difficult for them. They often moved in the spring, after school was out, with Detroit being a notable exception. They moved from Meaford to Detroit after school had already started and then moved from Detroit on to Tennessee halfway through the school year.

Before they moved from Meaford to Detroit, Gaston was offered the chance to be a missionary to Africa. Gaston had frequent correspondence with John Sherriff, a missionary in Mashonaland, Rhodesia. Gaston wrestled with the idea,[147] because he was very interested in spreading the gospel around the globe. Eventually, however, he turned it down, because  he was worried about how it would affect the girls.

He knew his frequent moves were hard on his daughters, but perhaps he didn't realize how hard. When they moved from Meaford, Verna vowed to herself to never again make close friends wherever they moved. Claire determined that someday, her children would have a home town to call their own.

Buy the Truth and Sell it Not

Chapter 15
Back to the States

In September 1929, a meeting was held in which it was decided to move the *Christian Monthly Review* magazine from Meaford to the home of the new editor, Lloyd G. Snure, in Hamilton, Ontario. Gaston Collins was leaving Meaford to live at 5755 Missouri Avenue in Detroit and become the minister at a "baby congregation"[148] in Dearborn, Michigan. A new church began meeting in August 1929 at the Robert Oakman School building on Chase Road in Dearborn. By the time Gaston became the preacher in October, there were eighty in attendance. Bible classes soon grew in attendance from 60 to 179. Sunday night meetings and cottage prayer meetings were begun, as well as a building fund.

Dearborn Church of Christ

Gaston was only there a short time, as he had agreed to fill the pulpit while the congregation waited on another preacher. Gaston found time to also preach some Sunday nights at the Vinewood church, and Ada found time to begin teaching three Chinese immigrants to speak English, along with helping her girls learn their lessons for their new school. Paul McAllister, writing a history of the congregation in 1934,

The Evangelist

said of Gaston, "He was with us for only a few months, but while here he and his family made a place in our hearts that will long be remembered."

Gaston loved his girls, but wished for a son to follow in his footsteps as a preacher. When Wilma had been born, he had even called her Billy for awhile, pretending that she was a son.[149] When the family left Canada, Gaston had the pleasure of helping a young man from Meaford named George Emptage to come to the states. George attended Harding College and became a naturalized citizen. He preached in Decatur, Alabama, Gainesville, Florida, Dayton, Ohio, Nashville, Tennessee, and Cordell, Oklahoma. Gaston thought of him as a son in the faith, and perhaps also as the preacher son he never had. Unfortunately, George had to leave the ministry after a few years due to health reasons.

Jean, Wes, Eleanor, & George Emptage

The family left Detroit on December 30 for Portland, Tennessee. For the girls, then young teens, moving from Canada to Tennessee was a big culture shock. They were frequently corrected in school for using British spellings such as plough and centre. (Gaston continued to use British spellings

House in Portland, Tennessee

such as Saviour and baptise.) The girls also found that girls and boys swimming together, which was common in Canada, was not allowed by Christian parents in Tennessee. On the other hand, going to worldly places like movie theatres, which was frowned upon in Canada, was not a problem in Tennessee.

As always, Gaston did not confine himself to just one congregation. He became the first preacher at the newly formed Fountainhead Church of Christ in Sumner County, three miles south of Portland, preaching there once a month. Gaston, forty years old that year, reported that during 1930 he had participated in seven meetings over 81 days, which resulted in 78 additions to the church. These included a 12 day meeting in Dunmor, Kentucky, a 16 day meeting at Bushes Chapel near South Tunnel, and meetings in Portland, at Rock Ridge near Portland, and at Mt. Pleasant, Tennessee. In some of these he was the preacher, and in some he was songleader with B.C. Goodpasture, Harold L. Olmstead and Robert H. Boll.[150] He received sad news at the end of the year. His college friend O.E. Tallman, with whom they had spent the Easter break two years earlier, died November 5, 1930.

A gospel preacher during this time rarely expected a lot of financial compensation for his service. Many congregations were poor and most preachers struggled financially like everyone else in the congregation. A

The Evangelist

preacher might hold a gospel meeting during which he received room and board from the members. At the end of the two week meeting, instead of cash, he might be given some produce from the members' gardens or perhaps a few live chickens. In spite of their limited resources, Gaston and Ada tried to enrich the girls' lives as much as possible. They took them to see the famous pianist Paderewsky on tour and the violin master Fritz Kreisler. They took them to see the Oberammergau Passion Play when it came to the Ryman Auditorium, and they went to many community concerts.

In 1931, Foy E. Wallace became the editor of the *Gospel Advocate* magazine. Foy knew Gaston, having stayed in his home when he had held a meeting in Meaford. Foy came to Portland and asked Gaston if he would become the office secretary of the *Gospel Advocate*. Gaston agreed, and the front page of the magazine on October 22, 1931 shows Gaston as the new office secretary and editor of the "Sowing and Reaping" column (a news and notes column). He stayed with the *Advocate* until 1937.

Buy the Truth and Sell it Not

Gaston moved the family to 1401 Beechwood Avenue in Nashville. They began worshipping at Waverly-Belmont Church of Christ at the corner of 12th and Beechwood. Gaston began sometimes leading singing and preaching for the congregation. On Saturday nights, the family would invite neighbors over for cake, homemade ice cream, and the singing of hymns, often with Ada or the girls accompanying on the piano. Years later, one of Gaston's friends would say that Gaston knew how to have a good time at a party.[151]

Beechwood Ave. house

Sometimes Gaston would string lights behind the house for his girls to have a backyard party with their friends. In an early version of speed-dating, the girls would have five minute dates with the boys attending. Verna remembers walking with Batsell Barrett Baxter down to Waverly-Belmont and sitting on the steps and talking during their five minute date.

Living in Nashville allowed Gaston to serve at many different churches in the area. In 1933 when the Boscobel congregation in East Nashville moved to Shelby Avenue and 17th Street, Gaston helped conduct services the first day in the new building.[152] The congregation at Joseph Avenue and Scott Street and the one at Grace Avenue and North 3rd Street (both in East Nashville north of Spring Street) listed Gaston as one of the preachers who served

Shelby Avenue

The Evangelist

there.[153] At some point, Gaston did a radio program with WLAC.

Joseph Avenue

Grace Avenue

Hillsboro

Radnor

The Hillsboro Church of Christ at the corner of Hillsboro Pike and Ashwood Avenue used Gaston as one of their monthly rotating preachers.[154] The Radnor Church of Christ (off Nolensville Pike south of Thompson Lane) had slow growth until 1935 "when E. Gaston Collins labored regularly with the congregation."[155] Gaston was always interested in steering young men on the right pathway. While at Radnor, Gaston wrote a one page tract entitled *Does it Pay to Go to Church?* that examined the effect of church attendance on society. It is reprinted in Appendix D.

In 1934, John T. Hinds, the new editor of the *Gospel Advocate* reprinted a booklet entitled "Around the Lord's

Buy the Truth and Sell it Not

Table." This had first been published by A.B. Lipscomb of the *Advocate* in 1917. The updated reprint included articles about the Lord's Supper by men all the way from Alexander Campbell to J.C. McQuiddy. Also included was an article entitled "Song Hints" by E. Gaston Collins. In it Gaston gave some brief comments about using songs as part of the Lord's Supper worship. He also provided a list of seventy-seven suggested songs, which are listed in Appendix E. There are several songs on this list that today are not usually considered to be Lord's Supper songs.

> (A personal note: This author, as a young man, was annoyed whenever a songleader would lead the song "Break Thou the Bread of Life" before the Lord's Supper. I then believed that this song has nothing specifically to do with the Lord's Supper, but instead compares the word of God to the loaves from the miracle of Jesus. Imagine my surprise when I read my grandfather's list of suggested Lord's Supper songs, and there on the list is "Break Thou the Bread of Life." I must study this more!)

In June of 1937, Gaston and family moved to Lawrenceburg, Tennessee to work with the Downtown Church of Christ. Gaston published that church's first bulletin. Gaston reported that it was "a wonderful church in many ways: a large membership, and one of the best houses I've seen among us. We have had some additions, and find much to do to encourage a large number of the careless."[156] In 1938, Gaston preached a 13 day meeting in Gallatin, Tennessee.

The Evangelist

H.L. Olmstead reported it as "Good attendance, good preaching, good spirits, and good results. Nine were baptized and three restored. Bro. Collins endeared himself to our people here by his spiritual messages and fine Christian spirit."[157]

Lawrenceburg bulletin

At Lookout Mountain

Ada, Gaston & Hallie Tallman

In 1938, Gaston, Ada and the girls took a trip to Florida, where Gaston preached in a meeting and they got to see their old friends, the O.H. Tallman family. In 1939, they took a trip to Nova Scotia, stopping at the Lincoln Memorial in Washington, the World's Fair in New York and in Concord, Massachusetts.

Buy the Truth and Sell it Not

Passenger lists show them returning from Nova Scotia to Boston on July 26, 1939 on the S.S. Yarmouth steamship.

Girls at Concord Bridge   **Gaston & Ada, Ferdie & Willie Steensland (Gaston's sister)**

Also in 1939, Gaston preached at a meeting in his old hometown. He reported, "The meeting in my old home of Huntland, Tennessee closed last Sunday night with good crowds, and five baptized. The house built over forty years ago is still in good condition, and, though small, the present membership is carrying on in a fine way."[158]

Gaston was still very protective of his grown daughters. In 1940, when *Gone With the Wind* opened across the country, Verna and her friend Dot Whitesell had a double date with Norvell Young and Batsell Barrett Baxter to see the midnight showing. Through a miscommunication, Gaston thought they were supposed to be *home* at midnight. When they finally got home, Gaston was furious. He sent Dot away, even though she was supposed to spend the night with Verna. He dismissed the young men and gave Verna a stern rebuke.

The Evangelist

Claire, Gaston, Wilma, Ada, Verna

Lubbock, Texas

In June of 1940, Gaston and Ada moved to Lubbock, Texas where he was associate minister with the Broadway Church of Christ. The regular minister, G.C. Brewer, was frequently away at meetings, requiring an associate minister. Gaston also did a radio program with KFYO.

On July 3, 1940, Gaston and Ada's oldest daughter, Claire, wed Griffin Cook at the chapel of Harding College in Searcy, Arkansas, with Gaston performing the ceremony. In December of 1940 Gaston turned fifty years old. In March of 1941, his father figure, Uncle Joe, passed away.

When Gaston and Ada left Lubbock, many in the congregation expressed their love and good wishes. Pansie and Mac McGuire wrote, "We shall always remember you as a very jolly couple." Ethel Newman wrote, "I've never known anyone 'shorter' and learned to love them 'longer and mucher.'"[159]

In 1942 Gaston and Ada moved to 1734 North Euclid Street in St. Louis, Missouri, where he preached for a year.

Buy the Truth and Sell it Not

In March of that year, Gaston and Ada's first grandchild, David Cook was born. In April, Gaston went to Canada to hold a meeting in Toronto, where he stayed with the Yates family. One of the Detroit churches considered him for a preaching position that year.[160]

From 1943 to 1945 Gaston and Ada rented a house at 1489 Woodmont Boulevard in Nashville and then bought a brick house at 1701 Green Hills Drive across from David Lipscomb College, paying $4000 for it.[161] Gaston served as Boys Work Secretary (activities director) for the YMCA. In June of 1943, he conducted the annual learn-to-swim campaign. With instructors from the Y staff and the Red Cross, 275 boys from 8 to 12 received free swimming lessons.[162]

Ada, Gaston, Billy & David

In August 1943 Gaston published a small folder encouraging Bible reading and giving a schedule for reading it in a year, shown in Appendix F. He said he had read the Bible through every year since 1924. A second grandchild, Billy (William Gaston) Cook, was born in March of 1945.

The Evangelist

From November 1945 to 1948 Gaston and Ada lived in Woodsfield, Ohio, where he preached at the "Old Brick" church building there. After a year there, Gaston reported:

> "Attendance and interest are good. We have recently started a men's training class which is proving helpful and interesting. The contributions are good. We have a good start on a Building Fund for a badly needed meeting house. Our present one is ninety years old – good for its age – but it is not at all adequate for any expansion, and successful class work. In addition to that the church recently bought a residence for the minister, paying $1500.00 down – balance on easy terms. We finally got possession, and are now living at home, after being here for eleven and one-half months. We are having fellowship with five different points in mission work and helping the orphans. Much more outside work, they tell me, we are doing now, than this church has ever done. We have had some additions to the work along through these months, and some better spirit is discernible – all-in-all good, considering the stormy sea through which the church has been sailing."[163]

Woodsfield, Ohio - Old Brick

Gaston and Ada's youngest daughter Wilma was married December 27, 1946 and divorced a short time later. Their oldest daughter, Claire Cook had their first granddaughter, Jane who was born in February of 1948. From 1948 to 1949, they lived in Ada, Oklahoma, where

Buy the Truth and Sell it Not

Gaston was the first preacher for a new congregation, the Southwest Church of Christ.[164] This was at least the fourth time in his life that Gaston had been the first preacher in a new congregation. He also conducted a Tuesday night Bible class at the colored Hammond Heights Church of Christ, and did a radio program on KADA.

1947 Christmas card

Southwest Church of Christ
Ada, Oklahoma building

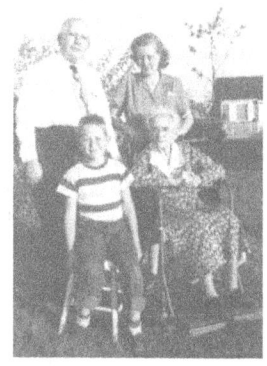

From 1949 to 1952, Gaston and Ada lived at 2819 Erica Place in Nashville. Gaston's mother Mamie lived with them there. In her later years Mamie had been in the habit of having a glass of wine before bed, but that practice came to a halt while she lived with Gaston. Gaston may have tried selling insurance during this time, as there were business cards printed in his name for the American National Insurance Company.

The Evangelist

Gaston preached in Mt. Pleasant, Tennessee, and also tried being a newspaper editor for a short time. From July 8, 1949 to January 26, 1950, Gaston was the first editor of the first newspaper in Goodlettsville, Tennessee, the *Goodlettsville Gazette*. The publisher, John L. Oliver, wrote many of the editorials for the paper, but Gaston's influence can be seen in such features as "Bible Comment" and "My Favorite Verse," as well as a newsy column he wrote called, "As I was telling Elmer...." While he was editor, the circulation increased from 2805 to 5246. No indication was given why he left the paper, just a sudden article announcing a new editor. Gaston also preached at the Robertson Fork Church of Christ.

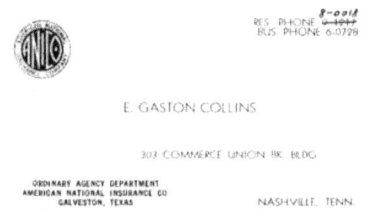

Mt. Pleasant church building

Buy the Truth and Sell it Not

In December of 1950, Gaston turned 60 years old. On December 20, Ada's mother, Ella Simm died in Nova Scotia. Gaston's mother Mamie died March 22, 1952 of circulatory failure and coronary disease at age eighty.

From 1952 to 1957, Gaston and Ada lived in Borden, Indiana. Their fourth grandchild was born in March of 1953. Gaston did radio programs with WGRC and WSLM.

A picture from the time shows Gaston at the nearby Pekin, Indiana Fourth of July celebration, which is the oldest continuous Fourth celebration in the nation.

Gaston helped organize Borden's first Vacation Bible School in 1954, with attendance as high as 150. A fund for a new building was begun while Gaston was there.[165] Ray Naugle from Borden remembers Gaston's fine singing, and that the first time he heard the songs *Come Ye Disconsolate* and *I'll Live for Him* was when Gaston led them.[166]

Gordon Trainor of Borden was married by Gaston in the preacher's home on Martinsburg Road. He surprised Gaston by giving him a hundred dollar bill for his service.[167] Les Wright remembers that Gaston was the preacher who baptized him at age 12, and that Gaston worked to get all the young people to sit together at the front on Sunday mornings. He also remembers that Gaston was good at stepping on toes that needed to be stepped on![168]

The Evangelist

Gaston loved studying the scriptures. There was a trying time in his life that probably motivated him to study false teachers. This resulted in an article he wrote about the "chiefest apostles" referred to in 2 Corinthians 11:5 and 12:11 by the apostle Paul.[169] This article is reprinted in Appendix G.

In 1957, Gaston and Ada moved to 236 South Court Street in Sullivan, Indiana, where they worked with the East Jackson Street Church of Christ. A newspaper in Sullivan reported that "Bro. Collins believes in being fair and honest with all; and most important, with the Word of the Lord. He insists upon the 'whole counsel of God' as an interpretation, and practice of a slogan of the early Churches of Christ, 'We speak where the Bible speaks, and are silent where it is silent.'" On April 22, 1957, Gaston bought the last house he and Ada would share, at 1107 Caldwell Lane in Nashville.

Section IV

Sell it Not

Buy the Truth and Sell it Not

Chapter 16
Warfare

The great tragedy of Gaston's life was not that his father died when he was five. It was not that he had to leave Nova Scotia, or that his friend O.E. Tallman died in his forties. It was not when divorce or scandal touched his family,[170] or later when he became legally blind. The great tragedy in the life of E. Gaston Collins was that he was viciously attacked by men who were supposed to be his brothers in Christ.

Many people originally were drawn to the Church of Christ because they did not like being told they must believe creeds that were not in the Bible. They did not like being told that they could not study and learn the Bible for themselves. For many people, unfortunately, the Restoration principles of "Speak where the Bible speaks," "No creed but Christ," "In matters of opinion, liberty," and "In all things, love," were smashed and rewritten like Orwell's *Animal Farm* rules. A critical moment in that process occurred in October of 1931.

We saw earlier that R.H. Boll was forced out of his position as editor of the *Gospel Advocate* in 1915 because of his views on premillennialism. Many of the early leaders of the Restoration Movement, such as Alexander Campbell and Walter Scott, believed in premillennialism, a literal thousand year period that was part of the Second Coming of Jesus. It was not a major issue with them, and certainly not something to divide Christians.

There was, however, often a very different attitude among premillennialists. Focusing on the second coming of Jesus often caused them to believe, as the first century

Sell it Not

disciples did, that Jesus is coming soon, and that there is a lost world that needs to know about the grace of God right now. Thus, the grace of God and the Great Commission were very important to them. Alexander Campbell even named his magazine the *Millennial Harbinger* because he believed the second coming should be our focus. As C.S. Lewis said, "Christians who did the most for the present world were precisely those who thought most of the next. It is since Christians have largely ceased to think of the other world that they have become so ineffective in this."[171]

Many people believe that premillennialism died out in churches of Christ because of a lack of scriptural evidence. This is not true. In fact, one of the leaders of the Restoration Movement, T.W. Brents, wrote about the millennium from Lewisburg, Tennessee[172] in his *Gospel Sermons* (published in 1891 by the Gospel Advocate Publishing Company). He made a convincing scriptural case for a literal millennium separating the first and second resurrection.[173] The subject, though, he said, was "not so important as that any one's salvation depends on a knowledge of it. A mistake concerning it, therefore, would be entirely harmless."[174]

Harmless, however, is not what some later leaders of the church thought about it. Many, Earl West said, "were completely convicted that premillennialism was a gross error, a denial of some fundamental teachings of the Scriptures, and a threat to the purity and purpose of the New Testament church."[175]

The millennium dispute was a particularly ugly period of church history. One side claimed that not only was premillennialism a gross error, but that it was on a subject that could not be completely understood, was unnecessary to salvation, and was divisive to the body. The other side claimed that if we want to "speak where the Bible speaks," we will study the whole counsel of God, not just convenient passages. We don't have to completely understand or agree on it, they said, but we should study it. The dispute saw many straw-man arguments, *ad hominem* attacks, and indictments of guilt by association.

Premillennialism died out in many churches of Christ in the twentieth century not for scriptural reasons, but because of the jackbooted verbal assaults on all who dared not oppose it. We cannot know the hearts of those who chose to do these assaults. Like the original sin in the Garden of Eden, some were deceived into believing they were doing the right thing. Some, like Adam, were not deceived, but went along with it. Others, like the serpent, were led by their own pride. Whatever motivated these men, they sold out the truth of God's Word to impose a millennium creed on the church that did irreparable harm to the gospel cause.

David Lipscomb was writing about older issues in the *Gospel Advocate* in 1908, but he could have been talking about the assault on premillennialism when he said, "There is no surer sign of the decline of interest in the great matters of obeying God and saving souls than to see professed Christians become greatly interested in minor and unimportant questions."[176] The idea that someone in the church must decide every minor point and that everyone in the church must fall in line with that belief not only dilutes our work on things that are truly important, but it also denies the freedom we have in Christ.

If we truly want to have "No creed but Christ," then we will neither be pre-millennialists, post-millennialists, nor a-millennialists, but "pan"-millennialists:[177] recognizing

Sell it Not

that everything at Christ's second coming will "pan" out according to God's will, regardless of what we think. We will then turn our attentions to the weightier matters of obeying God and saving souls.

Chapter 17
The Prayer

After R.H. Boll left the *Gospel Advocate,* he continued writing in the Louisville, Kentucky based *Word and Work* magazine. Many of the people who disagreed with him still considered him a member of their brotherhood. In 1927 R.H. Boll and H. Leo Boles had a debate about the millennium which ended amicably, with both sides agreeing to disagree. Gaston Collins first met Robert H. Boll in Toronto and had been associated with him as a songleader in meetings since then.

Waverly-Belmont building

Gaston as we've seen, was hired by Foy Wallace to work at the *Gospel Advocate* in September of 1931. Gaston was also asked by the Waverly-Belmont church to lead singing at a meeting which began September 27 of that year, with Clarence L. Wilkerson, of Springfield, Missouri preaching. The second night of the meeting R.H Boll attended, and Gaston, after consulting with the elders of the church, called on Boll to lead the prayer, which he did. After the service, both Foy Wallace and S.H. Hall, who were present, congratulated Gaston on having the courage to call on Boll for prayer. The next day in the offices of the *Gospel Advocate* , Foy told Gaston that he was "not all het up on the Boll matter." (colloquial for "not all heated up").

Sell it Not

The second week of the same meeting had a completely different outcome. On October 5th, F.B. Srygley was present at the service. Eleven years earlier, Srygley had been the victim of an outrageous commencement at David Lipscomb College that may have had some effect on what happened this week in 1931.

In 1920, John T. Lewis was the speaker at the David Lipscomb College commencement. He warned the graduates about not compromising their principles. Then he named the names of several men in the audience whom he claimed had compromised the truth, including Brothers F.B. Srygley, A.B. Lipscomb and several others. A few weeks earlier, there had been a meeting at a Christian church in town. In a spirit of Christian unity, these men had gone to the meeting, and had led a prayer or participated in the worship when asked. They were now being publicly condemned for it.[178]

There are many circumstances in life when we must speculate on "What Would Jesus Do?" Regarding conflicts with brothers, however, we know exactly what Jesus would have us to do, because He has told us. In Matthew 18:15-17, Jesus commanded a three step process for dealing with conflict with a brother. First, we are to go to the brother privately. At the conclusion of the October 5, 1931 service, F.B. Srygley did just that, approaching Gaston and strongly criticizing him for calling on Boll for prayer the previous week.

Jesus said that next, if the problem is not resolved, we should take two or three witnesses to talk to the brother. If that does not resolve the problem, then it should be taken to the church. There is no indication that Srygley tried to follow steps two or three of Jesus' commandment.

Buy the Truth and Sell it Not

Sadly, those who loudly proclaimed that they were trying to preserve sound doctrine in the church in the twentieth century often completely ignored Jesus doctrine and instead used gossip and public condemnations as their tools. Srygley apparently talked to Foy Wallace and within a few days, Foy became "all heated up" on the Boll matter. In 1933 and 1934, Foy had his famous fiery debates on premillennialism, and lines of disfellowship were drawn as people were forced to take sides. Srygley later admitted that those who opposed Boll had "too much personality in the fight." He never expressed regret at opposing Boll, but he did regret that those who had opposed Boll later began to fight among themselves.[179]

In one of his Hardeman Tabernacle Sermons entitled, "Is Christ with Us?" N.B. Hardeman (of Freed-Hardeman College) made this observation of the Restoration Movement:

> "They said: 'In our practice let there be nothing required of man other than that which is taught in the Bible, either by direct statement, or by approved example, or by necessary inference.' Those are the planks laid down, and then to guarantee the matter, they said, 'In all things of faith, let there be unity; in all matters of opinion, let there be liberty; in all things, let there be charity.' Friends, that's the only hope of this sin-cursed world; that's the only hope of healing the breaches in the religious world today."[180]

These were true words spoken by Brother Hardeman, but it is hard to read them and to imagine what he might have considered a matter of opinion, since in an earlier sermon he had attacked premillennialism and taken a swipe at Gaston:

Sell it Not

"It is characteristic of this cult to profess an extremely pious air, and to be negative on all questions, and not to try to expose any kind of an error, even in the sectarian and denominational world. They can put their arms around folks in error and honey them up, and say, 'Brother, kindly lead our prayer.' Now that's the spirit of it. There's the harm. It's the sacrifice brethren, of the old landmarks."[181]

Gaston Collins, to this author's knowledge, never preached a sermon on premillennialism. He never wrote a sentence in defense of it. He never even offered an opinion on it, but he was branded as a premillennialist because he was a friend of Robert Boll, he called on him for a prayer, and he refused to denounce him. In 1940, after Gaston had moved to Lubbock, Texas, the *Bible Banner* published an article deriding Gaston as "The Lubbock Substitute." In other articles, Gaston was accused of conspiring against Foy Wallace. Some of the attack language seems more suited to a cheap Hollywood western than to men who claim to follow the Prince of Peace.[182]

Friendships didn't count for much in the hysteria of the times as lines were drawn between people. In 1951 Gaston's daughter, Claire Cook, was approached by her preacher.[183] When asked, "Is your father a premillennialist?" she replied, "No, he's just a Christian." That answer did not satisfy him, and he decided to intervene at the Robertson Fork congregation where Gaston was preaching.[184]

Many congregations at the time did not have preaching every Sunday. A preacher might come once a month, and on other Sundays the congregation would have Bible school and a worship service without a sermon. Sometimes a member might make a few brief comments

Buy the Truth and Sell it Not

in place of a sermon, or the brother serving the Lord's Supper might make extended comments.

Robertson Fork Church of Christ is a thriving, historic congregation that has met in the same location since 1832. Gaston was hired by Robertson Fork in January 1950 to preach every first Sunday for one year. Evidently he was well liked because he continued preaching there in 1951 also. Church records show two members restored while he was there.

Robertson Fork Church building

In July 1951 Oaks Gowan held a meeting at Robertson Fork. Gaston had helped train Oaks to be a preacher when he was a boy in Lawrenceburg, but evidently Oaks had been told that Gaston was a premillennialist and he now snubbed him. Avis Wiggins of the Church Street congregation told the Robertson Fork elders they should fire Gaston because he was a premillennialist. One of the members objected that, "He never did preach anything like that."[185] One member at Robertson Fork remembers Gaston being let go because he was going to preach on premillennialism.[186]

Avis Wiggins had preached at Robertson Fork in the past and was the current minister of the largest church in the area, so he would have had some influence with the elders. No doubt the elders felt that because of all the current controversy in the church concerning premillennialism, that they should follow the safe course and dismiss Gaston. Church records for August 26, 1951

Sell it Not

say "A meeting of the elders and deacons was called to decide on whether or not to dismiss Bro. Gaston Collins as monthly preacher, as it was reported that he was a premillennialist. The vote was 6 to 2 in favor of dismissing him."[187]

The following Sunday, September 2, 1951, church records say, "A meeting of the elders and deacons was called. Bro. Collins was questioned on the millennial question and he would not take a stand. He was told that the vote was unanimous to dismiss him." Gaston no doubt felt he was being asked to "sign on the dotted line," as he later referred to it, on a question he believed was a matter of opinion and that he did not intend to preach about anyway, so he refused to answer.

Church records for the following Sunday say, "A meeting was called of the men of this congregation to let them decide with a vote whether to keep the preacher or not or whether or not to pay him for rest of year. It was decided not to keep him and pay him for the rest of the year."

Evidently, strong feelings were stirred up within the congregation. On the next Sunday, a petition that had been signed by twenty-nine men of the congregation was presented. It asked all officers of the Robertson Fork church to resign so there might be more harmony in the church. The congregation operated without elders for thirteen years, until October of 1964.

After being branded a premillennialist, Gaston likely had difficulty finding a congregation which would accept him. No doubt that is why he moved to Borden, Indiana, where the congregation was more open to the teachings of R.H. Boll.

Buy the Truth and Sell it Not

Gaston owned a copy of *How to Win Friends and Influence People* (printed in 1940), and it was Gaston's belief that the best way of serving the Lamb of God was by using the gentle approach. This suited his temperament. Other Christians with more fiery temperaments would do well to remember that our battle is not against flesh and blood, but against the devil. Their gifts would best be used to confront evil, instead of attacking people who are trying to follow Christ.

Gaston had hoped that brotherly love would prevail and that he would be reconciled with Foy and others who had attacked him. After twenty-four years, he saw that was not likely to happen, so he wrote a paper giving his account of what had transpired. Entitled "Hot A-Plenty by Now," it refers to the way Foy Wallace went from being "not all het up on the Boll matter" to "Hot A-Plenty." It is reprinted in Appendix H.

When R.H Boll died in 1956, Gaston paid tribute to him thusly:

> "In 1924 (or '25) I first met Brother Robert H. Boll. We were living in Meaford, Ontario and he was in a meeting in Toronto. About two weeks before his decease we last saw him a few minutes in the *Word and Work* office, when he greeted us in his usual, cordial manner. I was associated with him during the years in between, including a very pleasant time when I led the singing in one of his meetings at Mt. Pleasant, Tenn. Our association was consistently congenial, pleasant, and brotherly. He esteemed me (from first to last) a brother in Christ, as I did him. I thought his sermons were clear and forceful, his knowledge of the Bible amazing: and withal, he was sincere and humble before God. With an abiding faith I believe he loved God and His word supremely, accepting 'the whole counsel of God.'

Sell it Not

It seemed to me that he was always willing to let me be responsible for my own faith – not once did he (nor those associated with him) ever try to get me to sign on the dotted line, or sound me out to line me up on any particular item of faith or doctrine, to commit me to their views. To me, under certain trying circumstances, this idea of freedom in Christ, was most impressive and grew to be very precious." - E. Gaston Collins, Borden, Indiana.[188]

R.H. Boll

Buy the Truth and Sell it Not

Jesus in the Garden of Olives, by Gustave Dore

Sell it Not

Chapter 18
All Be One

On the night before He died, our Lord prayed that His disciples might all be one. Satan has been trying to keep that from happening ever since. If Christians are to learn anything from the millennium war of the twentieth century, we should learn that God hates division among His people.

Jesus gave the perfect model for Christians, which is also the perfect model for church fellowship, in Matthew 5:3-16:

> "Blessed are the poor in spirit: for theirs is the kingdom of heaven. Blessed are they that mourn: for they shall be comforted. Blessed are the meek: for they shall inherit the earth. Blessed are they which do hunger and thirst after righteousness: for they shall be filled. Blessed are the merciful: for they shall obtain mercy. Blessed are the pure in heart: for they shall see God. Blessed are the peacemakers: for they shall be called the children of God. Blessed are they which are persecuted for righteousness' sake: for theirs is the kingdom of heaven. Blessed are ye, when men shall revile you, and persecute you, and shall say all manner of evil against you falsely, for my sake. Rejoice, and be exceeding glad: for great is your reward in heaven: for so persecuted they the prophets which were before you. Ye are the salt of the earth: but if the salt have lost his savour, wherewith shall it be salted? it is thenceforth good for nothing, but to be cast out, and to be trodden under foot of men. Ye are the light of the world. A city that is set on an

Buy the Truth and Sell it Not

hill cannot be hid. Neither do men light a candle, and put it under a bushel, but on a candlestick; and it giveth light unto all that are in the house. Let your light so shine before men, that they may see your good works, and glorify your Father which is in heaven."

In verses 23 and 24 of the same chapter, Jesus tells us that being reconciled to our brother is more important than bringing a gift to the altar. Christians who follow these teachings will never have divisions.

In Mark 9:38-41 Jesus told His disciples that "he who is not against us is on our side." A wonderful example is given in Acts 15:37-40, where we see there were sharp contentions between Paul and Barnabus about Mark, and they each went their way serving God, but there was no division between them. We see later in II Timothy 4:11 that Paul called for Mark to come minister with him. They were still brethren, and each served God in his own way.

Jude 19 tells us that people who cause divisions don't have the Spirit of God. In Romans 16:17, Paul tells us to avoid those who cause divisions. In I Corinthians 1:10-25, he pleads that there be no divisions. In Galatians 2:11-21, Paul withstood Peter for creating a division between Jews and Gentiles. In I Timothy 6:3-10, Paul warns of those who are obsessed with disputes and arguments over words. In II Timothy 2:22-26, he says that "a servant of the Lord must not quarrel, but be gentle to all, able to teach, patient, in humility correcting those who are in opposition," In Titus 3:9-11, he said to "reject a divisive man after the first and second admonition."

Gaston very much believed in the "whole counsel of God," (Acts 20:27) and that all Scripture should be

Sell it Not

considered and studied, not just a few convenient verses. Continuing on in Acts 20 after encouraging "the whole counsel," Paul had warned the disciples at Ephesus against "savage wolves" who would come and try to draw away the disciples. Jesus Christ would later commend this same church for keeping out false teachers, but He also said He had something against them, that they had left their first love (Revelation 2:2-4). Perhaps they had fought with false teachers so much that anyone with a different idea became a false teacher to them.[189] Perhaps they had become weary of fighting and forgot why they initially became Christians. The battles fought between Christians over the years may have also caused many to lose their first love. If so, Christ's words also apply to us, "Remember therefore from where you have fallen; repent and do the first works," –Revelation 2:5

When Gaston Collins was editing the *Christian Monthly Review* in Canada, he wrote an article about "Scrappy Churches."[190] He said Christians often "scrap" over matters of opinion because they are not devoting themselves to the work of the Lord. As Galatians 5: 14-15 tells us, we need brotherly kindness and love, instead of biting and devouring one another. Otherwise, Gaston said, we may end up like the cats in this poem:

> There once were two cats in Kilkenny,
> Who each thought there was one cat too many;
> So they howled and they fit
> And they scratched and they bit
> 'Til, instead of two cats, there weren't any.

Section V

The Light Shines in Darkness

Buy the Truth and Sell it Not

Chapter 19
Going Home

In 1957, Gaston and Ada purchased the last home they would share on earth, at 1107 Caldwell Lane in Nashville. Gaston had grown up near David Lipscomb's boyhood home in Beans Creek, and now he would spend his final years near David Lipscomb's last home in Nashville. Nashville was a natural place for Gaston and Ada because they had served at so many churches and made so many friends there over the years. Two of their daughters lived nearby. On May 3, 1958 the youngest daughter Wilma married Ed J. Spicer and in June 1959, their second granddaughter, Barbara Spicer, was born. Their first great-grandchild, Susan Cook, was born in 1967. Their daughter Verna was married December 16, 1967 to Merl Thompson in Oklahoma City.

Gaston, Barbara, & Jane

Living close to David Lipscomb College also allowed Gaston and Ada to bring in a little income by renting out a room to students. They had a front room with a separate entrance and two beds for students. They let their oldest grandson, David, use half the room along with Tommy Sowell when he attended college there. Later, their second grandson, Billy used the room along with Bill Massey. Tommy and David gave Gaston the private nickname of

The Light Shines in Darkness

"Slick" because he was so good at catching them misbehaving.

There was a popular song at the time called "Sugar Shack" that Billy Cook and Bill Massey liked so much that they bought letters at a store and spelled out "Sugar Shack" on their front door. It didn't take Gaston long to catch it, and he told the boys in no uncertain terms that his house was not a Sugar Shack.[191] Another time Bill Massey was headed down the hall when he saw that Gaston was standing in front of Billy Cook, giving him a lecture about something. Cook was apparently not too chastised, as he gave Massey a wink as he passed.[192]

Gaston still did occasional preaching and holding meetings in the area. His granddaughter Jane was visiting once when Gaston and Ada were invited to a home for Sunday dinner. When they arrived at the home after Sunday morning service, the dinner was already set out on the table, where it had been waiting since that morning, covered with a tablespread. The mashed potatoes were cold and hard and the lettuce was wilted and flapping in the breeze of the room fan, but Gaston complimented the host on what a good meal it was and thanked her profusely.[193]

When not preaching somewhere, Gaston and Ada usually attended Central Church of Christ in downtown Nashville. Central had a large outreach ministry to the local community and also had a deaf ministry. Gaston had

Buy the Truth and Sell it Not

a deaf friend there, Mr. Pryor from Portland, with whom he enjoyed communicating by writing notes. After Gaston became blind, this process required an interpreter between them. Just as he had when he had worked at the YMCA, Gaston enjoyed encouraging young men. Now he sometimes visited the Lindsey Avenue Church of Christ Hobby Shop, where young men were given a place for wholesome activities.

Gaston never had a television. If the president addressed the nation, such as during the Cuban missile crisis, Gaston and Ada went to a neighbor's house to watch. Otherwise, they received their news by radio and newspaper. Gaston enjoyed several radio programs. If Paul Harvey was on, Gaston would "shush" everyone in the room so he could listen. Carl McIntire had a daily program entitled "The Twentieth Century Reformation Hour" in which he talked about moral decay in America, the spread of communism in the world, and apostasy in mainline churches. Billy James Hargis had a similar program entitled "Christian Crusade." Although McIntire had a Presbyterian background and Hargis came from the Disciples of Christ, Gaston would sometimes say of them what he also said about Billy Graham, "If he would let me offer the invitation, he could preach for me!"

In 1963, the *Nashville Banner* did a story on Gaston and Ada's fiftieth wedding anniversary. In it, Gaston's last preaching assignment was given as Ardmore, Alabama.[194] Gaston preached at so many places over the years that it's impossible to know them all. Places

The Light Shines in Darkness

like Valdosta, Georgia; Bardstown, Kentucky; Atwood in Carroll County, Tennessee; Beersheba Springs and Gruelti-Laager in Grundy County, Tennessee; Mitchellville, Corders Crossroads, and Thompson's Station in Tennessee; Paint Rock and Oxford Schoolhouse in Alabama; and places in Mississippi were all on his preaching schedule. Throughout his life the Great Commission took him to twelve states and three provinces.

Gaston began losing his sight in the 1960s. There was no treatment for detached retina at that time, and though Gaston had a little bit of vision, he was legally blind and could 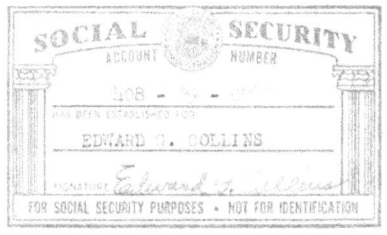 not read or drive. After he lost his vision, his granddaughter Jane helped him organize many of his papers and files he had collected over the years. He briefly considered buying a house in Lewisburg where Claire could be of more assistance to them, but decided against it. He did buy some land in Marshall County, Tennessee, but it was only to hold it until his son-in-law could afford it.

When this author would visit Gaston, I would read the newspaper to him. When the *Nashville Banner* was delivered in the afternoon, he would have me read each headline, and if it interested him, he would have me read the story. One day there was a front page story about a panty raid that had taken place at Vanderbilt University the night before. As a shy pre-teen boy, I was embarrassed to even read the title to him, and I was really surprised when he asked me to read the article. When I finished the

Buy the Truth and Sell it Not

story, he didn't make any comment, just gave a very slight chuckle. I suppose it amused the mischievous boy that was still inside him.

He could be mischievous at times. He thought that all telephone wrong numbers were either pranks, or else the result of someone being too lazy to look up the number, and therefore, fair game for his own prank. When someone would call and ask for someone who was obviously a wrong number, he would say, "Just hold the phone." Then he would lay the receiver down on the table and go about his business. Sometime later, he would go back and hang up his phone.

Sometimes he might mock people a little bit. When the garbage man came around and asked if there were any "gaa-bige", he might reply that he had no "gaa-bige." He didn't mind making fun of himself either. He captioned a picture of himself in downtown Nashville, "*A 'sight' sight-seeing on Church St.*" He laughed at the time he accidentally had the camera turned the wrong way, looking through the lens instead of the viewfinder, and took a whole roll of pictures of his face.

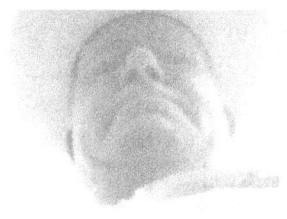

Gaston invents the Selfie

The Light Shines in Darkness

Socrates said the unexamined life was not worth living, and Gaston certainly believed in self-examination. During the 1960s, civil rights demonstrations and legislation were much in the news, and Gaston once asked this author if I thought black people and white people should marry. As a young boy, I had given very little thought to civil rights or to marriage in general, and none at all to inter-racial marriage. I thought a moment and then said, "Well, I guess it's okay if they love each other."

What's interesting to me, thinking back on that conversation, is that even though inter-racial marriage was still illegal in many states, and preachers of many different denominations were preaching that it was a sin, Gaston did not tell me what *I* should think, or even what *he* thought about the issue. He knew it was an issue that the church of my generation would have to deal with, and I believe he wanted me to examine my own thoughts.

In 1965, Gaston organized a clean up of his family cemetery in Huntland. Relatives were recruited for the labor, along with a family friend, Houston Williams. This author drew the easy assignment of scribe, and a picture from the time shows Gaston dictating while I made notes. Gaston later typed up this list in a report about the cemetery.[195] It is included in Appendix I.

Gaston tried his best not to let his blindness slow him down. He still wrote letters to his family, like Paul, writing with his own hand in

Buy the Truth and Sell it Not

large letters. He may have produced a booklet on Baptism during this period. He still occasionally preached entirely from memory. He had friends, daughters, grandchildren, and his great-nephew Bill Steensland to drive him places. Once he preached completely from memory at the Bluff Springs congregation in Marshall County, and relied on this author to read Scriptures at various points during the lesson. He loved singing, and his beautiful tenor voice had deepened into a melodious bass in his old age. When the congregation sang *In the Sweet By and By*, you would clearly hear his "By and By" in the bass part.

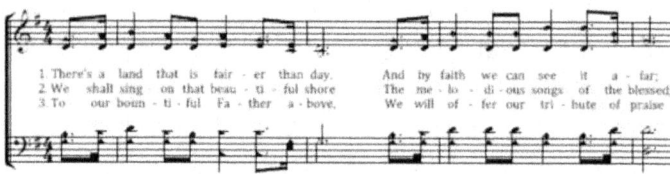

The Light Shines in Darkness

In 1968, Gaston and Ada celebrated their 55th wedding anniversary with a three week trip to Nova Scotia.[196] Their lives had literally gone from the days of the horse and buggy through the age of trains and then automobiles and finally, on this trip, to jet planes. In Nova Scotia, they had their picture made in front of the house Ada would have lived in if she had married a local man. Instead, she lived in many houses over the years wherever the Great Commission led Gaston.

David. Frank. Billy.
Barbara. Ada. Gaston & Jane

Buy the Truth and Sell it Not

After Gaston stopped driving, he and Ada still attended Central Church of Christ in downtown Nashville, relying on a neighbor for transportation. Occasionally, they would instead walk to Granny White Church of Christ nearby. Once when walking home from an evening service at Granny White, Gaston commented on the closing song that had been sung, *Am I a Soldier of the Cross?* "That song has real meaning," Gaston said, and Ada, not realizing that the comment was probably intended for my edification, replied, "Well, of course it has meaning." Gaston was perhaps thinking of something he had written years before in *Unequal Yoking*, that the Christian should devote himself completely to God, just as a soldier devotes himself to his country.

On the wall outside his home office, Gaston had a framed copy of a *Nashville Tennessean* cartoon from January 21, 1934, drawn by the famous cartoonist Joseph L. Parrish. In it, a man representing *Befuddled Mankind* is

The Light Shines in Darkness

holding up a puny lantern representing *The Material* and standing amid *Worldly Fears and Uncertainties* saying "I'm Lost!" Behind him is an image of Jesus representing *The Spiritual* saying "I am the Light of the World." The caption says "Maybe We are Depending Too Much on the Wrong Light."

This cartoon calls to mind the fifth verse of the first chapter of the Gospel of John, "And the light shineth in darkness, and the darkness comprehended it not." Neither physical darkness in the form of blindness, nor spiritual darkness in the form of attacks were ever able to extinguish the light of Jesus inside Gaston.

In his prayers, Gaston would sometimes pray for "this poor old world." I imagine that when he did, he had the general fallen condition of the world in mind. Also, I imagine he was thinking of those people who claim to be Christians, but through their pride have caused divisions in the church. Gaston didn't care much for prideful men. He told his daughter once, "I never licked anyone's boots!"[197]

Gaston's shoe stand , for shoe shining, not boot-licking!

Buy the Truth and Sell it Not

The Light Shines in Darkness

Chapter 20
The Unclouded Day

Preachers perform a lot of funeral services. Gaston had a Cokesbury Preachers Manual that gave him general guidelines for a funeral. Each service is different, of course, tailored to the individual. This is particularly true when the preacher knew the deceased well.

In 1948, Gaston performed the funeral for Mrs. R.E.L. Taylor. She had been born Tennessee Ann Hawk and had been baptized by the same preacher who had baptized Gaston, James K. Hill. She and her husband were in the grocery business in Decherd, and perhaps Gaston got to know them at the grocery after high school each day, or perhaps later when the family lived with Gaston's mother in Decherd. They kept in contact through the years, and Gaston tells of visits in later years, "For the last eleven years Sister Taylor was in failing health, and suffered much from arthritis, which gradually grew worse, in spite of many efforts for relief. On my visits with her I found her mind clear and her thin, drawn fingers busy with needlework as she sat in the wheel chair. She retained a lively interest in the work of the church, always asking about my work and family and of the work of others. She bore her constant suffering bravely and patiently. I found her uncomplaining and resigned by the grace of God to carry her burden."

When Gaston performed her funeral service, he said, "I talked about The Unclouded Day, and showed that whereas she had come through much physical suffering here, she could look for something far better where the spirits of the just are made perfect and freed from suffering in the land that is fairer than day."[198]

Buy the Truth and Sell it Not

Gaston's funeral was Sunday, March 8, 1970. He died at age 79 on March 6, 1970, and Ada survived him until May 4, 1978. Like his father, Gaston died of a nosebleed or stroke. At Gaston's funeral, Brother Thomas Whitfield said that Gaston loved the truth and stood for what he believed, in spite of popular opinion. In a letter to her children, Claire Cook said of Gaston's love of the Bible, "I have never met anyone who loved and revered it more than your granddaddy."

Gaston's sister Mollie with Ada

The Light Shines in Darkness

The Apostle Paul's letter to the Romans in chapter 10, verse 15 quotes the prophet Isaiah, who said, "How beautiful are the feet of those who preach the gospel of peace." Gaston Collins' feet went many places preaching because he loved the truth, loved God's Word, and loved telling the good news of the gospel of peace to as many people as he could.

- The End -

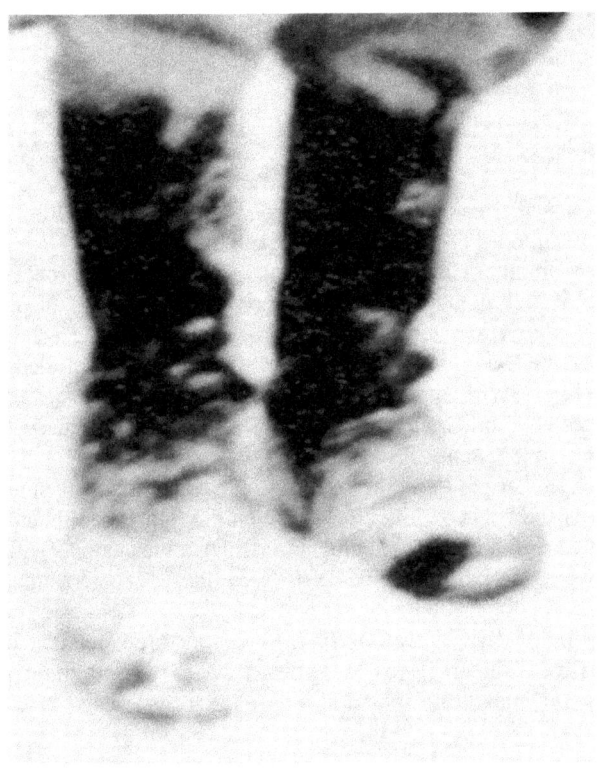

Detail from Gaston's photo on p. 45

Buy the Truth and Sell it Not

Endnotes

Chapter 1 – Beans Creek

[1] James C. Taylor, *Franklin County, Tennessee and Settlers in the Early 1800's,* (1991), p.68.

[2] Evelyn Rogers, *Focus on Franklin County,* (1966), p.11.

[3] Jessie A. Henderson, "Unmarked Historic Spots of Franklin County," *Tennessee Historical Magazine,* (1934), Series II, Vol. III, pp. 111-120.

[4] Sarah Hunt Moore, "A Brief History of the Salem Church of Christ to 1900," *Franklin County Historical Review,* (June 1974), p. 24; also Jim Hargrove, *Interesting Moments in the History of Huntland and the Surrounding Area,* (2003), p. 101.

[5] John N. Lovett, Jr., (2010), *Falls Mill,* p.5.

[6] *National Banner and Nashville Whig,* (July 11, 1828).

[7] Eastin Morris, "Salem," *Tennessee Gazetteer,* (1834).

[8] Proceedings of the State of Tennessee, 22nd General Assembly, 1837-1838.

[9] Gert Petersen, *David Crockett, The Volunteer Rifleman,* (2007), p. 10.

[10] Henderson, pp. 111-120; Hargrove, p. 10.

[11] His grandmother Collins maiden name was Elizabeth Barbee, spelled with two e's, but in his War of 1812 records, he signs with one e.

[12] *Membership Roster and Soldiers, Vol.I, 1894-1960,* The Tennessee Society of the Daughters of the American Revolution, compiled by Edythe Rucker Whitley, (1961), p. 1668.

[13] "Tennessee Land Grants in Vicinity of Salem Located/Surveyed in 1807," Franklin County TN Historical Society.

[14] Keith Cemetery in Franklin County, south of Huntland, Tennessee.

[15] Records show that Collin's men were on the right side of General William Carroll's line, where the main British attack came. (U.S. Dept. of the Interior, Jean Lafitte National Historical Park, New Orleans)

[16] Hargrove, p. 7.

[17] Bob Hilliard, *Dear Hearts and Gentle People,* (1949), music by Sammy Fain. Different singers have used different lyrics to apply to their own hometown. Dinah Shore's version referred to Tennessee.

The Life of E. Gaston Collins

Chapter 2 – The Matriarch

[18] Robert E. Hooper, *Crying in the Wilderness: a biography of David Lipscomb,* (1979), p. 16.
[19] *Membership Roster and Soldiers, Vol. II, 1960-1970,* The Tennessee Society of the Daughters of the American Revolution, compiled by Edythe Rucker Whitley, (1970), p. 276.
[20] Earl West, *The Life and Times of David Lipscomb,* (1987), p. 21.
[21] Robert Neville Mann and Catherine Cleek Mann, *Lipscomb Family Manuscripts,* (1953), p. 21.
[22] *Ibid.* This information is not in the original text, but in a marginal note of the copy in Lipscomb University's Beaman Library Special Collections. It was probably added by a later family member, possibly Houston Lindley. Several houses and communities in Virginia bear the name Mt. Airy. The palatial home of the Tayloe family in Richmond County, and the home of the Leftwich family in Bedford County, Va. are possible inspirations for the name.
[23] A nearby house in Franklin County (on Mingo Road) is nearly identical to Mt. Airy and has been remarkably well-preserved. Possibly it was built first - perhaps by George Vanzant about 1826, and later lived in by Granville Lipscomb. Source: Joy Q. Gallagher, "The Simmons-Weddington House," *Historical Tidings,* (October 2010), Vol. 42, No. 4, p.2, Franklin County Historical Society.
[24] K.M. Van Zandt, *Force Without Fanfare: The Autobiography of K.M. Van Zandt,* (1968), p. 59. Major Van Zandt was Ann Lipscomb's grandson. The other three grandsons in college at the same time were Will Collins, Garland Lipscomb, and Ira Lipscomb.
[25] Howard M. Hannah, *Confederate Action in Franklin County,*(1992),p.1.
[26] Robert E. Hooper, *Crying in the Wilderness: The Life and Influences of David Lipscomb,* (2011), p. 64.
[27] Michael R. Bradley, *Nathan Bedford Forrest's Escort and Staff,* (2006), pp. 126-7.
[28] "Bedford County - Dr. Thomas Lipscomb," *The Goodspeed Histories of Tennessee,* (1972), p. 1160.
[29] Hannah, p. 12
[30] "Union Provost Marshal's File of Papers Relating to Two or More Civilians," National Archives, Washington, D.C., (Microcopy 416, Roll 50, Records 12783, 13980).
[31] West, (*Lipscomb*) p. 21; also Hargrove, p. 133, (Hargrove says he was hung. West says he was shot.)

Buy the Truth and Sell it Not

[32] Military Map Showing the Marches of the U.S. Forces Under the Command of Major General W.T. Sherman, 1865, Tennessee State Library and Archives map # 34271.
[33] Brigadier General Vincent J. Esposito, USA (Ret.), The West Point Atlas of American Wars, (1959), I, Map 109.
[34] Southern Claims Commission, (1880), No. 12084, Ofc. 218, Report 10, Status: Denied. Also, W.L. Collins, Administrator, reported to the County Court on July 17, 1891 that he had been unable to collect a claim against the U.S. Government in the name of Mrs. Ann D. Lipscomb. Source: 1890's file #992, Project Preservation, Winchester, TN.
[35] W.L. Moore, (letter to E. Gaston Collins, Dec. 16, 1946).
[36] Annie Hunt Moore and David Lipscomb, *Gospel Advocate,* (1870), pp.401-2. The birth date of 1778 in this obituary and in some books is believed to be wrong, as it contradicts her tombstone (1779), Goodspeeds History (90 years old), DAR records (1779), and David Lipscomb's account of Yankees invading on her 84th birthday.

Chapter 3 – Old Salem
[37] Hooper (2011), p. 16.
[38] West, (*Lipscomb*), p.27
[39] West, (*Lipscomb*), p.28
[40] Hooper (1979), p. 25.
[41] E.M. Forster, "Only connect…live in fragments no longer…," *Howards End,* (1910), Chap.22.
[42] Hebrews 4:12.
[43] Granville Q. Lipscomb, *David Lipscomb,* (paper, Peabody College, 1938), p. 2.
[44] Accounts vary slightly between David Lipscomb (*Gospel Advocate,* 1867, p.584), Granville Q. Lipscomb, Earl West, and Robert Hooper, some referring to the wife as Ann and some as Nancy (Nancy Ann?), and varying in number of children (Most likely it was one boy and twin girls, all infants).
[45] West, (*Lipscomb*), p. 28.
[46] Sarah Hunt Moore, "Salem," p. 25.
[47] Buddy Reynolds, of the Old Salem congregation, 2013.
[48] The devastating effects of the war both upon the unity of the church and on the Lipscomb family no doubt helped form David Lipscomb's belief that a Christian should remain separate from civil government as much as possible. See *Civil Government* by David Lipscomb (1889).

The Life of E. Gaston Collins

[49] Tennessee Census of 1860, Franklin County record #87-110.
[50] Hargrove, p. 108, says that an 1873 fire destroyed much of Salem, and that "Collins & Co," had losses of $115. There were receipts for William L. Collins receiving spirits at Hunt's Station in July and August of 1873 and postage stamps in July of 1895. These were recorded by the author in an inventory of Claire Collins Cook's documents. Original documents are now lost.
[51] E. Gaston Collins, *Collins Cemetery Association,* located in Appendix I. Also, Franklin County records show that William L. Collins bought 270 acres for $2524.50 on April 1, 1871 (Franklin County Project Preservation 1870's record #840).
[52] E. Gaston Collins, "News and Correspondence," *Christian Monthly Review,* (Nov. 1928), p. 12.
[53] *Ibid.*
[54] West, (*Lipscomb*), p. 12. We know that David Lipscomb was at Old Salem at least once while Gaston was there, holding a meeting there in 1901 when Gaston was ten. Even when not present, Lipscomb's spirit and teachings infused the entire congregation.

Chapter 4 – De Troubles of de World

[55] West, (*Lipscomb*), p. 1.
[56] Arthur C. Hill, *The History of Black People in Franklin County, TN,* (thesis, University of Minnesota, 1981), p.57.
[57] Michael R. Bradley, "The War Taught Him to Love Horses," *It Happened in the Civil War,* (2010), p. 148.
[58] Bradley, *Nathan Bedford Forrest's Escort and Staff,* (2009), p. 137.
[59] Hill, p. 41.
[60] E. Gaston Collins, "An Even Temper," *Christian Monthly Review, (April 1926), p. 8.*
[61] J.B. O'Neal, *Soldier's Application for a Pension* #6905, State of Tennessee, Huntland, Franklin County, (March 28, 1905).
[62] Sarah Hunt Moore, "Hunt's Station, Hunt, Huntland, Tennessee: Its Early History," *Franklin County Historical Review,* (June 1974), p. 31; also R.L. Polk, "Huntland," *Tennessee Gazetteer and Business Directory,* (1887, 1890) lists I.B.[sic] O'Neal as one of two blacksmiths in town.
[63] Cause of death of W.L. Collins is unknown. Joe Collins later reported to the County Court that he paid $15 to Dr. J.W. Grisard of Winchester for medical services for W.L. Collins. Source: 1890's File #325, Project Preservation, Winchester, TN.

Buy the Truth and Sell it Not

[64] 1900 census of Franklin County, Tennessee.
[65] E. Gaston Collins, "As I Was Telling Elmer...," *Goodlettsville Gazette*, (Nov. 3, 1949), p. 3.
[66] W. Claude Hall, "News and Correspondence," *Christian Monthly Review*, (Nov. 1926), p. 11.
[67] E. Gaston Collins, obituary of H.R. Moore and Annie Moore, *Gospel Advocate*, (Sept. 21, 1933), p. 904.

Chapter 5 – The Iron Horse

[68] T.F. Rhoton, *A Brief History of Franklin County, Tennessee*, (thesis, University of Tennessee, 1941), p.27.
[69] Claire Cook, obituary of Gaston Collins, *The Christian Visitor*, (January 1975).
[70] Verna Thompson, (phone interview Feb. 6, 2013).
[71] E. Gaston Collins, "As I Was Telling Elmer...," *Goodlettsville Gazette*, (Dec. 1, 1949), p. 3. This lantern today is in the possession of David Cook.
[72] The Threm Faucet Company remained in business until the 1960's, at which time it donated its remaining samples to the Forestry Dept. of the University of the South at Sewanee, where they remain on display.
[73] Claire Cook, obituary of Gaston Collins, *The Christian Visitor*, (January 1975).
[74] E. Gaston Collins, "Editorials," *Christian Monthly Review*, (June 1927), p. 4.

Chapter 6 – The Remarkable Tallmans

[75] Geoffrey Ellis, *The Maritime Bible and Literary College*, (paper of the Canadian Churches of Christ Historical Society, Aug. 15, 2009), pp. 4-7.
[76] Ellis, p. 14.
[77] *Ibid.*
[78] West, (*Lipscomb*), p. 12. David Lipscomb warned against extremes.
[79] Gwen Lefton, *The Wallace Family*, (1983), pp. 67, 80.
[80] E. Gaston Collins, "Editorials," *Christian Monthly Review*, (June 1927), p. 4.

Chapter 7 – College Years

[81] Gwen Lefton, *West Gore*, (1987), p. 62.
[82] Thomas C. Whitfield, Gaston's funeral service, March 8, 1970.
[83] David Cook interview.

The Life of E. Gaston Collins

[84] Verna Thompson, (phone interview Dec. 11, 2012).
[85] Lefton, *West Gore,* p. 103.
[86] Ellis, p. 24.
[87] Ellis, p. 55, Also, Canadian Churches of Christ Historical Society Facebook post (November 19, 2013).
[88] *The Bible Student,* (May 1913), p.7.

Chapter 8 - Ada
[89] Claire Cook, letter to Verna Thompson, (Aug. 23, 1975).
[90] Ada's passport application, (May 13, 1918, Washington, D.C,)
[91] Gaston's draft registration, *World War I Selective Service Draft Registration Cards 1917-1918,* National Archives and Records Administration, Franklin County, TN, Roll # 1852983.
[92] Gaston probably didn't get his singing ability from the Lipscomb side of the family; David Lipscomb once said of himself that he had trouble distinguishing the tune of *Nearer My God to Thee* from that of *Dixie.* (Granville Q. Lipscomb, p. 5).
[93] Verna Thompson, (phone interview Feb. 4, 2013).
[94] The size of the surviving print (4-5/8 x 3-1/2) suggests it may have been taken with a #3 Brownie camera, one of the mass-marketed line of Brownie cameras which sold for $4. The size of several later photos was 2-1/4 x 3-1/4 inches, suggesting perhaps a Folding Pocket Kodak camera, which sold for a whopping $10.

Chapter 9 – The Attack
[95] R. Vernon Boyd, *A History of the Stone-Campbell Churches in Michigan,* (2009), p. 135.
[96] Boyd, p. 115.
[97] This quote is actually a popular paraphrase of Augustine of Hippo's quote that for a Christian, "truth belongs to his Lord."
[98] Boyd, p. 167.
[99] Ellis, p. 36.
[100] Ellis, p 34.

Chapter 10 - Survival
[101] State Teachers College, Murfreesboro, Tennessee transcript (1915).
[102] Claire Collins, *Autobiography,* (paper from Portland, TN High School, 1931), reprinted in Appendix B.

Buy the Truth and Sell it Not

[103] The U.S. Railroad Administration did not take over the railroads until 1917, but before that time war shipments and labor strikes caused many disruptions. Also, boat passages were restricted because of the submarine threat, especially after the May 1915 sinking of the *Lusitania*.

[104] As a veteran, he received a tombstone supplied and paid for by the government

[105] Gaston's daughter Claire once told the author that her father had worked at the faucet factory, but whether it was during his high school years or during these survival years, or both is unknown.

[106] Verna Thompson, (phone interview Jan. 8, 2013).

[107] Claire Collins, *Autobiography*.

[108] *Ibid.*

[109] From the author's inventory of Claire Collins Cook's papers. Original document has since been lost.

[110] Claire Collins, *Autobiography* says they lived on the streetcar line in Huntsville. The census of 1920 confirms this, showing them living in a rental house in Ward 4 of Madison County, Alabama.

[111] Batsell Barrett Baxter and M. Norvell Young, *Preachers of Today, Volume Two,* (1959), pp. 84-5.

[112] "Preaching at the Church of Christ," *Huntsville Daily Times,* (Oct. 5, 1919), p. 7.
"Society News," *Huntsville Daily Times,* (Nov. 14, 1919), p. 4.

[113] E. Gaston Collins, obituary of Cassie Stephenson Carlisle, *Gospel Advocate,* (April 1, 1920), p. 326.

Chapter 11 – Algood, Lipscomb, and Bridgeport

[114] Claire Collins, *Autobiography*.

[115] Verna Thompson, *The First Christmas I Remember,* (Christmas letter Dec. 16, 2009)

[116] *Ibid.*

[117] H.R. Moore, "History of Old Salem Church," *Gospel Advocate,* (Oct. 12, 1922), p. 962.

[118] *Backlog,* David Lipscomb College, (1923), p. 109.

[119] David Lipscomb College, Nashville, Tennessee transcript (1923).

[120] Claire Collins, *Autobiography,* reprinted in Appendix B.

[121] This piano, made in 1892, is now in the home of Billy Cook.

[122] *Word and Work,* (July 1924), p. 196.

[123] E. Gaston Collins, Unequal Yoking or Be not unequally yoked with unbelievers, (1924)

The Life of E. Gaston Collins

[124] E. Gaston Collins, "Letters," *Christian Leader, (October 23, 1923),* p.3.

Chapter 12 – Meaford by the Bay

[125] Border crossing records don't list Claire with the family, but Verna Thompson said this was an omission; the whole family was together. On July 21, 1925 Gaston obtained his minister's license for Meaford, Ontario. (Inventory of Claire Cook's documents; original document lost.)

[126] Verna Thompson, (phone interview Mar. 24, 2013)

[127] The chair today is in the home of Jane George. The Sessions mantel clock, bought from M.H. Huss Jewellers in Meaford, is today in the home of the author.

[128] Verna Thompson, (phone interviews Feb.28 and Mar. 31, 2013).

[129] E. Gaston Collins, "News and Notes," *Word and Work,* (May 1927), p.134.

[130] E. Gaston Collins, "News and Correspondence," *Christian Monthly Review,* (August/September 1927), p. 16.

[131] R.H. Boll, "News and Notes," *Word and Work,* (April 1928), p.102.

[132] This throw is today in the possession of Jane George.

[133] Claire Collins, *Autobiography*

Chapter 13 – The Editor

[134] D. McDougall, "The Ontario Annual Meeting," *Christian Monthly Review,* (July 1926), p. 7.

[135] E. Gaston Collins, "In Memoriam," *Christian Monthly Review,* (Mar. 1926), p. 18.

[136] E. Gaston Collins, "The Scriptural-Measure Life," *Christian Monthly Review,* (May 1926), p. 14.

[137] E. Gaston Collins, "Ideals – or Ideals of Life," *Christian Monthly review,* (July 1926), p. 20.

[138] *Ibid.*, p.21

[139] E. Gaston Collins, "Ideals – or Ideals of Life," *Christian Monthly Review,* (Aug. 1926), p. 12. I cannot locate the source of the quote he used; I've seen it attributed to later people, but not the original source.

[140] E. Gaston Collins, "Improving a Divine Arrangement," *Christian Monthly Review,* (June 1927), p. 5.

[141] E. Gaston Collins, "How to Advance the Evangelisation of Ontario," *Christian Monthly Review,* (July 1928), p. 4.

Buy the Truth and Sell it Not

[142] E. Gaston Collins, "Editorials," *Christian Monthly Review,* (May 1929), p. 4.
[143] E. Gaston Collins, "Remarks," *Christian Monthly Review,* (June 1929), p. 13.

Chapter 14 – The Father

[144] Verna Thompson, (phone interview Feb. 5, 2013).
[145] Richard Martindale of the East Jackson Street Church of Christ in Sullivan, Indiana (letter to the author Feb. 23, 2013)
[146] Verna Thompson, (phone interview Feb. 5, 2013).
[147] E. Gaston Collins, "News and Correspondence," *Christian Monthly Review,* (Nov. 1929), p. 14. He has just moved to Detroit, but says he is considering another important move.

Chapter 15 – Back to the States

[148] *Ibid.*
[149] Verna Thompson, (phone interview October 21, 2013).
[150] E. Gaston Collins, "News and Correspondence," *Christian Monthly Review,* (Oct. 1930), p. 14.
[151] Said to Alison Cook by a man in a wheelchair at the visitation for Misty Ezell George on December 1, 2009. Perhaps it was Jim Bill McInteer?
[152] "Homecoming Opens," *Gospel Advocate,* (Sept. 28, 1933)
[153] Joe Ridley, "Grace Avenue Church," *Gospel Advocate,* (Dec. 7, 1939), p.1153.
[154] J.E. Cotton, "Hillsboro Church," *Gospel Advocate,* (Dec. 7, 1939), p.1163.
[155] "Churches of Christ in Nashville," *Gospel Advocate,* (Dec. 7, 1939), p.1164
[156] E. Gaston Collins, "News and Notes," *Word and Work,* (February 1938), p.28.
[157] H.L. Olmstead, "News and Notes," *Word and Work,* (November 1938), p.237.
[158] E. Gaston Collins, "News and Notes," *Gospel Advocate,* (October 5, 1939), p.945.
[159] From a Remembrance address book given to Ada and Gaston when they left Lubbock.
[160] Boyd, p. 181.
[161] Verna Thompson, (phone interview October 21, 2013).

The Life of E. Gaston Collins

[162] Ridley Wills II, *The YMCA of Middle Tennessee*, (2011), p. 112.
[163] E. Gaston Collins, "News and Notes," *Word and Work,* (December 1946), p.280.
[164] "Church News," *The Ada Evening News,* (Dec. 24, 1948).
[165] E. Gaston Collins, "News and Notes," *Word and Work,* (January 1955), p.22.
[166] Ray Naugle, phone interview, November 12, 2013.
[167] Gordon Trainor, e-mail, November 16, 2013.
[168] Les Wright, e-mails, November 12-15, 2013.
[169] E. Gaston Collins, "Who Were the 'Very Chiefest Apostles'?" *Word and Work,* (April 1955), pp. 78-80.

Chapter 16 - Warfare

[170] Wilma suffered a divorce. Gaston's sister Mollie, in 1910 married at age 16 and had a baby three months later. One of Gaston's O'Neal uncles, John Robert, was sheriff, but another, Wade, was a bank robber, and another, Bill, committed suicide.
[171] C.S. Lewis, *Christian Behaviour: A Further Series of Broadcast Talks* (1944).
[172] For many years, a picture of Dr. Brents hung in the vestibule of the Church Street Church of Christ in Lewisburg.
[173] T.W. Brents, "The Millennium," *Gospel Sermons,* (1891), p. 339.
[174] *Ibid.*, p.325.
[175] Earl West, *The Search for the Ancient Order,* (1987), IV, p.176
[176] David Lipscomb, "The New Years Work", *Gospel Advocate,* (1908), p.8
[177] "Pan"-millennialist was suggested to me by Larry Clinkenbeard of Spring Hill, TN.

Chapter 17 – The Prayer

[178] Ottis L. Castleberry, *He Looked for a City*, (1980), pp. 245-6
[179] F.B. Srygley, *Gospel Advocate,* (August 31, 1939), p.813.
[180] N.B. Hardeman, *Hardeman's Tabernacle Sermons,* (1938), IV, p. 229.
[181] Hardeman, p.162-3. This quote was still being repeated in 1985. (William Cline, *Firm Foundation*, June 11, 1985, p. 5)
[182] Foy E. Wallace, "The Lubbock Substitute," *Bible Banner,* referenced in Claire Cook's letter to her children (January 18, 1984); In a later article, Foy accused Gaston of conspiring against him. He quoted his brother Cled Wallace, "The Judaizers and their sympathizers cannot meet

Buy the Truth and Sell it Not

Foy in debate and they would like to kill him." Source: "Repercussions From the Smear Campaign," *Bible Banner,* (July/August 1944), p.35-36
[183] Avis Wiggins of the Church Street Church of Christ, Lewisburg, TN.
[184] Claire Cook (letter to her children Jan. 18, 1984); also, Gaston is listed as one of the preachers at Robertson Fork, (G.W. Stallings, *Robertson Fork Church of Christ Directory,* 1989, p. 4)
[185] Claire Cook, (letter to her children, January 18, 1984).
[186] Clevland Holder, Phone interview with Mrs. Holder, (October 17, 2013).
[187] Robertson Fork Church of Christ Record 1947-1964, Microfilm #965, Tennessee State Library and Archives.
[188] Robert H. Boll obituary, *Word and Work,* (May 1956), p. 115.

Chapter 18 – All Be One
[189] Rick Rolin of Lewisburg, TN suggested this correlation in his evening sermon March 10, 2013.
[190] E. Gaston Collins, "Scrappy Churches," *Christian Monthly Review,* (Nov. 1928), p. 4.

Chapter 19 – Going Home
[191] Billy Cook, (phone interview Mar. 25, 2013).
[192] Bill Massey (interview Apr. 7, 2013)
[193] Jane George interview, 2013.
[194] *Nashville Banner,* (Oct. 18, 1963)
[195] Gaston referred to this cemetery as the Collins Cemetery. Other resources refer to it as the Lipscomb cemetery. There is another Lipscomb cemetery nearby, so this one would probably best be referred to as the Collins-Lipscomb cemetery. The cemetery has been cleaned of underbrush by David Cook at least once since the 1965 clean-up, but like most old cemeteries, it needs regular care.
[196] Bob Bell, Jr., "Churches Are News" column, *The Nashville Banner,* (October 19, 1968), p. 9.
[197] Claire Cook, (letter to her children Jan. 18, 1984).

Chapter 20 – The Unclouded Day
[198] E. Gaston Collins, obituary for Tennessee Ann Hawk Taylor, *Gospel Advocate,* (Feb. 10, 1949), p. 92.

The Life of E. Gaston Collins

Illustrations

Cover Artist --Nancy S. Hilgert
           http://www.fineartbynancyhilgert.com
Frontispiece---Edwin Gaston Collins, family photo
p. xii ---------Beans Creek, author photo
p. 1 -----------Jesse Bean, Franklin Co. Hist. Society
p. 2 -----------Stagecoach, Franklin Co. Hist. Society
p. 4 -----------Collins' tombstone, Alison Cook photo
p. 4 -----------Salem map, Franklin Co. Hist. Society
p. 5 -----------Ann Lipscomb, family photo, enhanced by
           Joe McGee, Smyrna, TN.
p. 6 -----------Ann's daughter, from *Force Without Fanfare: the Autobiography of K.M. Van Zandt*
p. 9 -----------Mt. Airy, author photo
p. 10 ----------Ann's tombstone, author photo
p. 14 ----------Old Salem, Franklin Co. Hist. Society
p. 17 ----------David Lipscomb, Gospel Advocate Publishing
p. 17 ----------Podium, www.therestorationmovement.com
p. 19 ----------William Lipscomb Collins, family photo
p. 22 ----------*It's Me O' Lord*, www.smallchurchmusic.com
p. 24 ----------Gaston at Huntland Academy, family photo
p. 25 ----------Annie Hunt Moore, Falls Mill, Huntland, TN
p. 26 ----------Locomotive, Franklin Co. Hist. Society
p. 27 ----------Franklin Co. High School, Franklin County Historical Society
p. 27 ----------L&N Decherd Depot, courtesy of the Tennessee State Library and Archives: Tennessee Rail Road Depot Photograph Post Card Collection. Image has been altered from the original to remove cars and power lines.
p. 28 ---------Oil lantern, author photo
p. 28----------Gaston at Huntland High School, family photo

Buy the Truth and Sell it Not

Illustrations

p. 28	---------	Cedar faucets, Jim Hargrove via www.heraldchronicle.com (Winchester, TN)
p. 29	---------	Composition book, family document
p. 30	---------	Canadian flag, via www.wikipedia.org
p. 32	---------	O.H. Tallman, Canadian Churches of Christ Historical Society Facebook page
p. 32	---------	O.E. Tallman, via ccchs.ca
p. 35	---------	Maritime Bible and Literary College, Canadian Churches of Christ Facebook page
p. 36	---------	College announcement, family document
p. 39	---------	Maple Leaf Quartet, family photo
p. 40	---------	Maple Leaf Quartet names, family photo back
p. 42	---------	Ada Simm, family photo
p. 43	---------	Lorenzo Dow Simm, family photo
p. 43	---------	Daddy Simm's store, family photo
p. 44	---------	Wedding photo, family photo
p. 45	---------	Gaston at falls, family photo
p. 45	---------	1st house + original water system, family photo
p. 46	---------	West Gore church, Canadian Churches of Christ Historical Society Facebook page
p. 48	---------	*An Open Letter*, from *The Maritime Bible and Literary College,* by Geoffrey Ellis, p.60.
p. 49	---------	Four generations in West Gore, family photo
p. 50	---------	Evangeline stamp, via Canadian Postal Archives online
p. 53	---------	J.B. O'Neal tombstone, DeLois O'Neal Thompson photo
p. 54	---------	Draft registration, National Archives, WWI Selective Service, Franklin Co., TN
p. 55	---------	Verna and Claire, family photo
p. 56	---------	Verna and Claire, family photo

The Life of E. Gaston Collins

Illustrations

p. 57 ----------Dallas Church, AL, via www.rison-dallas.com
p. 58 ----------Algood, TN house, family photo
p. 58 ----------Ada and girls in Algood, family photo
p. 61 ----------Mamie, family photo
p. 62 ----------Greek Club, 1923 *Backlog,* Lipscomb Univ. Beaman Library Special Collections
p. 62 ----------Preacher Club, *Backlog,* Lipscomb Univ.
p. 63 ----------Quartette, *Backlog,* Lipscomb University
p. 63 ----------The Havalind Acts, *Backlog,* Lipscomb Univ.
p. 63 ----------Debate team, *Backlog,* Lipscomb University
p. 64 ----------Bridgeport, AL church bldg., family photo
p. 65 ----------The girls in Bridgeport, family photo
p. 65 ----------Public Gardens of Halifax, family photo
p. 65 ----------Gaston at the dock, family photo
p. 65 ----------Ed Lloyd house, Bridgeport, family photo
p. 66 ----------Gaston on the mountain, family photo
p. 67 ----------*Unequal Yoking* cover, family document
p. 68 ----------Meaford Church of Christ, family photo
p. 68 ----------Meaford bldg. 12-2-13, Paul Linn Dale
p. 69 ----------The girls in Meaford, family photo
p. 70 ----------The girls at Meaford house, family photo
p. 70 ----------Verna, Ada, Gaston & Wilma, family photo
p. 70 ----------The Meaford house 12-2-13, Paul Linn Dale
p. 71 ----------Sledding, family photo
p. 71 ----------One-horse open sleigh, family photo
p. 73 ----------The family in Meaford, family photo
p. 73 ----------Mamie, Otoshige Fujimori, Ada, family photo
p. 74 ----------*Christian Monthly Review* cover, Canadian Churches of Christ Hist. Society, via ccchs.ca
p. 78 ----------Gaston, Ada and family, family photo

Buy the Truth and Sell it Not

Illustrations

p. 80 --------- Gaston in car, family photo
p. 81 --------- Mr.& Mrs.John Sherriff, Mashonaland, Rhodesia, family photo
p. 82 --------- Dearborn Church of Christ, family photo
p. 83 --------- George Emptage, Kirkwood Photographers
p. 83 --------- Portland, TN house, family photo
p. 84 --------- Gaston, Fountain Head, TN Church of Christ
p. 85 --------- Gaston, courtesy of *Gospel Advocate*
p. 86 --------- Beechwood Ave. house, family photo
p. 86 --------- Shelby Ave. church bldg., *Gospel Advocate*, December 7, 1939
p. 87 --------- Joseph Ave. church bldg., *Gospel Advocate*
p. 87 --------- Grace Ave. church bldg., *Gospel Advocate*
p. 87 --------- Hillsboro church bldg., *Gospel Advocate*
p. 87 --------- Radnor church bldg., *Gospel Advocate*
p. 88 --------- Lawrenceburg, TN bldg., *New Testament Churches of Today, Vol. 1*
p. 89 --------- Lawrencburg Bulletin, Downtown Church of Christ, Lawrenceburg
p. 89 --------- at Lookout Mountain, family photo
p. 89 --------- with Hallie Tallman, family photo
p. 90 --------- Girls at Concord Bridge, family photo
p. 90 --------- visit from Aunt Willie, family photo
p. 91 --------- Graduation, family photo
p. 91 --------- Lubbock, TX church bldg., *New Testament Churches of Today, Vol. 1*
p. 91 --------- Gaston, family photo
p. 92 --------- Gaston, Ada and 2 grandsons, family photo
p. 93 --------- the "Old Brick" church building, Woodsfield Ohio Church of Christ
p. 94 --------- Gaston and Ada, family photo

The Life of E. Gaston Collins

Illustrations

p. 94 ----------1947 Christmas card, family document
p. 94 ----------Ada, Oklahoma church bldg., Southwest Church of Christ
p. 94 ----------Four generations, family photo
p. 95 ----------Insurance card, family document
p. 95 ----------Church building, Mt. Pleasant Church of Christ
p. 95 ----------Newspaper letterhead, family document
p. 95 ----------Newspaper clipping, family document
p. 95 ----------*Goodlettsville Gazette*, Tenn. State Library and Archives, newspaper microfilm
p. 96 ----------Gaston in Indiana, family photo
p. 97 ----------Gaston Collins, family photo
p. 97 ----------Ada Collins, family photo
p. 98 ----------Holy Bible, Thomas Nelson, Inc., Nashville, TN, author photo
p. 104 --------Waverly-Belmont church bldg., *New Testament Churches of Today, Vol. 1*
p. 108 --------Robertson Fork church bldg., author photo
p. 111 --------R.H. Boll, *Word and Work* magazine
p. 112 --------Detail from *Jesus in the Garden of Olives* by Gustave Doré, Belford-Clarke Co., Chicago
p. 115 --------Two cats, *The Big Book of Nursery Rhymes,* illustrated by Charles Robinson, Blackie & Sons Ltd., London
p. 116 --------*I'm Lost,* Joseph L. Parrish, *Nashville Tennessean,* January 21, 1934
p. 118 --------Gaston and two granddaughters, family photo
p. 119 --------Gaston and Ada, family photo

Buy the Truth and Sell it Not

Illustrations

p. 120 -------- Gaston and Ada, Central Church of Christ, Nashville, directory photo
p. 121 -------- Social Security card, family document
p. 122 -------- Gaston on Church St., Nashville, family photo
p. 122 -------- Accidental self-portrait, family photo
p. 123 -------- Collins-Lipscomb Cemetery, family photo
p. 124 -------- *Sweet By and By,* words by Sanford F. Bennett, music by Joseph P. Webster, 1868
p. 125 -------- Trip to Canada by air, family photo
p. 125 -------- Foster Brison house, family photo
p. 125 -------- Gaston & Ada with grandchildren, family photo
p. 126 -------- *Am I a Soldier of the Cross?,* words by Isaac Watts, music by Thomas A. Arne, 1721
p. 127 -------- Shoe shine stand, author photo
p. 128 -------- *Unclouded Day,* words and music by Josiah K. Alwood, 1890
p. 130 -------- Gaston & Ada's gravestone, Woodlawn Cemetery, Nashville, author photo
p. 130 -------- Mollie and Ada, family photo
p. 131 -------- Boots, detail from Gaston's picture on p.45
Appendix F -- *To Read the Entire Bible in Twelve Months,* family document

The Life of E. Gaston Collins

Bibliography

Backlog. Nashville: David Lipscomb College, 1923

Baxter, Batsell Barrett and M. Norvel Young. *New Testament Churches of Today, Vol. One.* Nashville: The Gospel Advocate Company, 1960.

Baxter, Batsell Barrett and M. Norvel Young. *Preachers of Today, Vol. 2.* Nashville: The Gospel Advocate Company, 1959.

The Bible Student. Beamsville, Ontario.

Boyd, R. Vernon. *A History of the Stone-Campbell Churches in Michigan.* Southfield, MI, 2009.

Bradley, Michael R. *It Happened in the Civil War.* Guilford, CT: Globe Pequot Press, 2002.

Bradley, Michael R. *Nathan Bedford Forrest's Escort and Staff.* Gretna, LA: Pelican Publishing, 2006.

Bradley, Michael R. *With Blood and Fire.* Shippensburg, PA: Burd Street Press, 2003.

Brents, T.W. *Gospel Sermons.* Nashville: Gospel Advocate Publishing Co., 1891.

Canadian Churches of Christ Historical Society, Facebook page and website, www.ccchs.ca

Castleberry, Otis L. *He Looked for a City.* Marion, IN: Cogdill Foundation Publications, 1980.

Center for Restoration Studies, Abilene Christian University, www.bible.acu.edu

Christian Leader. Cincinnati, Ohio.

Christian Monthly Review. Meaford, Ontario.

Christian Visitor. Memphis, Tennessee.

Ellis, Geoffrey. *The Maritime Bible and Literary College.* Beamsville, Ontario: a paper presented to the Canadian Churches of Christ Historical Society, 2009.

Buy the Truth and Sell it Not

Esposito, Brigadier General Vincent J. *The West Point Atlas of American Wars, Vol. 1.* New York: Praeger Pub., 1959.

Family Histories of Franklin County, Tennessee. Paducah, KY: Turner Publishing Co., 1996.

Franklin County TN Historical Society, Facebook page and website, www.franklincountylibrary.org

The Goodspeed Histories of Tennessee. Chicago: Goodspeed Publishing Company, 1886. Columbia, TN: Woodward and Stinson Printing Co., 1972.

Gospel Advocate. Nashville, Tennessee. also Facebook page and website, www.gospeladvocate.com

Gospel Advocate obituaries, via therestorationmovement.com

Hannah, Howard M. *Confederate Action in Franklin County.* Winchester, TN: Winchester Historical Society, 1992.

Hardeman, N.B. *Hardeman's Tabernacle Sermons, Vol. IV.* Nashville: Gospel Advocate Co., 1938.

Hargrove, Jim. *Interesting Moments in the History of Huntland and the surrounding area.* Huntland, TN: 2003.

Henderson, Jessie A. *Tennessee Historical Magazine, Series II, Vol. III.* 1934.

Hill, Arthur C. *The History of Black People in Franklin County, TN.* Minneapolis: University of Minnesota, 1981.

Historical Tidings. Winchester, TN: Franklin County Historical Society.

Hooper, Robert E. *Crying in the Wilderness: a biography of David Lipscomb.* Nashville: David Lipscomb College, 1979.

Hooper, Robert E. *Crying in the Wilderness: The Life and Influences of David Lipscomb.* Nashville: Lipscomb University, 2011.

Lefton, Gwen. *The Wallace Family.* West Gore, Nova Scotia: 1983.

The Life of E. Gaston Collins

Lefton, Gwen. *West Gore to 1950.* West Gore, Nova Scotia: 1987.
Lipscomb, David. *Civil Government: Its Origin, Mission, and Destiny, and the Christian's Relation to it.* Nashville: Gospel Advocate Publishing, 1889.
Lovett, John N., Jr. *Falls Mill: A Legacy of Power and Industry.* Huntland, TN: 2010.
Mann, Robert Neville and Catherine Cleek Mann. *Lipscomb Family Manuscripts.* 1953.
Moore, Sarah Hunt. *Franklin County Historical Review Vol.V, No.2.* June, 1974.
Petersen, Gert. *David Crockett, The Volunteer Rifleman.* Winchester, TN: Franklin County Hist. Society, 2008.
Rhoton, T.F. *A Brief History of Franklin County, TN.* Knoxville: University of Tennessee thesis, 1941.
Rogers, Evelyn. *Focus on Franklin County.* Winchester, TN: 1966.
Taylor, James C. *Franklin County Tennessee and Settlers in the Early 1800's.* 1991.
Van Zandt, K.M. *Force Without Fanfare: The Autobiography of K.M. Van Zandt.* Ft. Worth: Texas Christian University Press, 1968.
West, Earl Irvin. *The Life and Times of David Lipscomb.* Germantown, TN: Religious Book Service, 1987.
West, Earl Irvin. *The Search for the Ancient Order, Vol. IV.* Germantown, TN: Religious Book Service, 1987.
Whitley, Edythe Rucker. *Membership Roster and Soldiers.* Tennessee Society of the Daughters of the American Revolution, 1961, 1970.
Wills, Ridley II. *The YMCA of Middle Tennessee.* Nashville: Dunham Books, 2004.
Word and Work magazine, Louisville, KY, Facebook page and website, www.wordandwork.org

Appendix A

My Last Railway Journey

by E. Gaston Collins
(from his high school composition book)

Aug. 10th of this year was a bright and sunny day.

Although the morning was thwarted by the burial of one of my relatives, I gave the evening over to jollity.

The Huntland base-ball team had a game with the Kelso team, the game being played at Kelso.

I was given the position of left fielder, so you see I had to be there.

I boarded the train going west at a little after one o'clock.

We were, as boys will do on an occasion like this, at the rear end of the train in a short time, talking, laughing, and waving at all who were near the track.

The landscapes were beautiful, - fields of ripe grain skirted about by belts of forests still green with the leaves of summer.

We were soon at Elora, and changed cars.

Thence we passed through Flintville, and Brighton, and soon we found ourselves in the hurrying, hustling little town of Kelso.

We had a cold drink, then went to the scene of the encounter.

The score stood decidedly in favor of Kelso, after the game.

My Last Railway Journey

We went back to town, for the train which was going toward home, was nearly due.

In a little while we were quietly seated in the gloomy looking car, in the place of calling vociferously other peoples attention to us.

Appendix B

Autobiography

Claire Collins

(This was an assignment when I was a junior in High School in Portland, TN. Mary Elizabeth Baskerville was the teacher.)

I was born (as I have been told, and firmly believe) in the little village of West Gore, Nova Scotia in "the Land of Evangeline." I only lived here about a year, when I left with my parents for Tennessee, by way of St. John, New Brunswick, Montreal, Toronto and Niagara Falls, but this view of the Falls I do not remember.

We lived for awhile, on reaching Tennessee, in Huntland. Here my sister was born and I was no longer the "only child."

When I was about 3 years young we boarded the train for Chattanooga, Tennessee. We lived in St. Elmo, a suburb, at the foot of Lookout Mountain. In about five months time we took a trip to Nova Scotia which I remember only a little. We went on the train by Washington to New York, then by boat up Long Island Sound to Boston. I can barely remember sitting on the deck of the ship and looking out over the water. This was during the War when there were submarines in the ocean so we went the rest of the way by train, instead of the usual boat trip from Boston to Yarmouth, N.S.

We spent the summer here, and on returning South we moved to Huntsville, Alabama. My youngest sister was born here and "now we are three." We played house with the neighborhood children, made mud pies, and put pins in certain shapes on the street car line that ran in front of

Autobiography of Claire Collins

the house, and when the street car ran over them they would be mashed together in this shape.

The next move was to Algood, Tenn. And to explain for all the moving, perhaps I had better say here that my father is a minister. This was only a small town but I'll always remember it because I started school here and never have I felt so big before or since.

After staying four years in this place, we must needs move again to Alabama, and this time to Bridgeport. It is situated at a bend in the Tennessee River and the scenery is very pretty. The main part of town is situated some distance from the river and we used to visit a girl friend who lived in a very pretty place near the river. We always "dressed up" in fancy clothes when we went there and had a wonderful time pretending we were "somebody." Then we would just be ourselves and sit on the stone fence that surrounded the yard, and eat peaches from the peach orchard.

We spent about a month in the summer on Cumberland Mountain about three miles from Bridgeport. There were about twenty little cottages at this place, and in front of them was "The Bluff," a large flat rock projecting out from the mountain. Here we had picnics and made bonfires at night and toasted marshmallows. The scenery from the bluff was beautiful. You could see for miles and miles and the Tennessee River looked like a tiny stream winding along the valley.

A little distance behind the cottages were springs of sulphur and iron water, and many people spent the summer here for the benefit of the water.

The second summer we were in Bridgeport, we made another trip to Nova Scotia. We left as soon as school was

Appendix B

dismissed in the Spring, going by train as far as Norfolk, Virginia. From here we took the boat to Boston. It took about two days and a half to make the boat trip as there was a terrible fog the second night and the boat stood still all night blowing the fog horns for fear of running into another ship. Nearly everyone (including ourselves) slept soundly all night and knew nothing of the danger they were in.

The dining room was down on a level with, and partly below the water and until we got used to it, it made us feel kind of "fainty" when we first went down.

I don't know what we would do crossing the ocean, for even on this short trip we became impatient for land to come into sight. But finally, about noon of the second day we saw a faint outline of the shore, and that afternoon the ship steered into Boston Harbor. We stayed two or three days in Boston with my Aunt and Uncle before taking the boat for Yarmouth, N.S.

This boat trip was very pleasant. It does not take quite twenty-four hours to make the trip. On reaching Yarmouth we took the train, which went along the coast. The scenery is magnificent along here. There are many apple orchards, and every now and then a glimpse of the ocean is caught from the train. Halifax was the next main stop and then we went almost due north for about forty miles (almost across the peninsula) until we reached "West Gore." We were very glad to find our grandparents well and happy and I enjoyed seeing the little village and the little grey house where I was born, although I had seen it before but did not remember it much. My grandfather owned a store and we certainly enjoyed "clerking" in the store that summer.

Autobiography of Claire Collins

My grandmother had a large tent pitched in the grove of trees at the side of her house and there were four beds in it. We slept here every night except two or three when there was a bad storm. Once there came a storm in the middle of the night and we all became so frightened we flew up to the house in our nightclothes, through the rain.

My Aunt, Uncle, and cousin from Halifax spent a good deal of the summer here and one day we and our cousin were at a neighbor girl's, who had a creek running through her fathers place. It was very hot so we decided to go in swimming and didn't bother going home for our bathing suits. When we did get home though you should have heard the "Wells!" and we were stripped and sent to bed for the rest of the day, and our clothes hung on the line to dry. That was a lesson.

Blueberries are to this section as strawberries are to Portland, but they grow wild, and all along the roads through the village. We went on several blueberry picnics. We left early in the morning and everyone picks until noon, when lunch is spread, and such a spread! And how it is enjoyed after working all morning.

My oldest sister and I spent a week in Halifax with my Aunt. We enjoyed this week immensly, swimming almost every day in the ocean and sight-seeing. The "Public Gardens" of Halifax were a special attraction. It would take several days to see everything as they cover such a large area. We managed to take about a dozen pictures here by the flower-beds, fountains and miniature lakes, in spite of the many "keep-off-the-grass" signs.

After we returned to West Gore, one day they prepared to motor up to Grand Pre' and other places around. There was not room for everyone, and my grandmother was

Appendix B

staying anyway to keep the store, so I (unselfish soul), volunteered to stay with her, thinking it would be fun to clerk in the store by myself while my grandmother kept house. But I have been sorry ever since because they saw many interesting places in and around Grand Pre'.

Our visit in "The Land of Acadia" was fast coming to an end so we prepared to leave again for the Southland. We took an affectionate leave of our grandparents for we did not know when we would ever see them again.

We went on the train north-west, through Evangeline Land. The traingoes right through Grand Pre' and you can see the chapel where the men and boys gathered to hear the command of the British. We saw also the well of Evangeline. I had not at this time read the beautiful poem "Evangeline" and could in no way appreciate seeing these. At Yarmouth we again took the boat to Boston and again the train through New York, Washington, Chattanooga and home. But not to be home for long, for again we prepared to move and this time to Meaford, Ontario Canada. I remember how I disliked the idea of moving so far and leaving all my friends and all the way up they kept asking me if I was going to Meaford and I said "No!" but I finally changed it and said "I suppose I'll have to." But I love it now and would love to return.

Before we got into Canada Mother said "Now girls, you must not say I done this and I done that because they don't say it there." I don't think we said it once. I guess we wanted to make a good impression on Daddy's congregation.

Meaford is a very pretty town and is situated on Georgian Bay, a part of Lake Huron, and in the chain of Great Lakes.

Autobiography of Claire Collins

The people, young and old, go in for sports summer and winter. In summer it is swimming, fishing, boating and picnicing. Almost everyone who can afford it builds a summer home on the Bay shore, where they spend about three months in the summer. I spent a part of the time with a girl friend who lived in the summer at "Kiwana Beach," about three miles up the Bay from Meaford. We spent the time swimming (mostly), and hiking up to the next beach "Sunnyside."

One of the main attractions to tourists is the fishing. It is called "trolling" as you let out several hundred feet of wire with a hook on the end and it trails along behind the boat. A silver cup is given each year to the tourist catching the largest fish and the largest I remember being caught weighed about forty pounds. The sea gulls feed on the intrals of the fish, which are thrown to them.

The snow that fell the first Christmas we were there astonished us. Snow ploughs went over all the side-walks early in the morning and in a short time you could not tell that they had been around.

We got skates and learned to skate the first winter, but not without many times bumping the ice. Often they had skating parties at the rink and sometimes the whole church would have one. All the mothers and fathers would get out their skates because this was usually about the only time during the year that they went.

There were many skiing, tobaganning, snow-shoeing and sleigh-riding parties held on the hill just above our house. It is certainly thrilling to go whizzing down a hill in the crisp night air on a bobsleigh or toboggan, together with a crowd of girls and boys, singing, laughing and

Appendix B

yelling. Then "simply starving," go to one of their homes to eat hot soup, crackers, sandwiches, and hot cocoa.

One Easter Holiday my parents, myself and youngest sister motored south as far as Hamilton, St. Catherines and Niagara Falls, Ontario. We stayed most of the time in St. Catherines with relatives. It is a very pretty city on the Willand Canal, and is sometimes called the "Garden City of Ontario."

Two carloads of us took lunch one day and motored to Niagara Falls and surrounding places of interest. On the way to the Falls we passes "Queenston Heights" famous for the war of 1812. On these heights a monument is erected in memory of General Brock, a British soldier who fought. Inside this monument were winding steps and we paid the guard at the door and climbed to the very top. We got very "winded" and had to stop to rest several times. We could look through small windows and the scenery was beautiful on all sides. On the way winding down we counted the steps and there are two hundred forty-five. A little piece over is also a monument to Laura Secord, a woman famous in this war because she carried a message twenty miles on foot and saved the British troops. We then proceeded to Niagara Falls. When we were in the city of Niagara Falls, driving along the river to the Falls we could feel the spray and of course long before this we could hear its mighty roar.

When the Falls came to view I was silenced because I could think of no words to describe its grandeur. We went over to it as close as possible and gazed and gazed. But finally we were reminded that it was noon and we drove to a quiet park and ate our lunch and made plans for the afternoon. They tried to arrange it so we could see the Falls at night when it is illuminated, but could not.

Autobiography of Claire Collins

We went up the river to the Whirlpool where the "basket" goes back and forth over it and carries people.

"Lundy's Lane" was a little town famous for the war 1812 and we saw the grave of Laura Secord.

We stayed only a few days longer at St. Catherines and returned to Meaford as the Easter holidays were over. I graduated from grade school that spring, or I passed the "Entrance" as the last year in grade school is there called. There are no graduation exercises or anything, neither in grade school or high school, and we received our diplomas through the mail.

About the 28th of August we attended the Canadian National Exhibition in Toronto which is about one hundred twenty miles south of where we were living. It is held annually for about two weeks and covers an immense area along the Lake front, and is just like a city within a city. Every year millions of people visit there, both from Canada and United States. We had seats in the huge grandstand and saw many wonderful performances and at the last, the fireworks. There was a large imitation castle and this appeared to be destroyed by fire.

The next day the lady's Marathon Swim took place. Swimmers from all over the world are in training all year to go in this swim. We didn't see anything like all there was to see as we did not stay quite two days.

We returned home again and in a few days school opened and I was a high school student. We were not called Freshmen but were in the "first form." I had ten subjects in all. I passed all my subjects this term but in the summer we moved to Detroit, Michigan and I began my second year in Northwestern High, Detroit. It is a very large school, consisting of about forty-five hundred pupils

Appendix B

(including several hundred negroes) and about one hundred sixty-five teachers. There are three buildings on the grounds and on the first two floors they are connected by long tunnels. There are ten graderooms (five for boys and five for girls). Mine was called Mt. Vernon House, 109. I went here the first day and got my list of subjects from the graderoom teacher. But my first class wasn't until 11:15 o'clock. When the time came I started looking for my Math room, 369. I wandered up and down halls and through tunnels and was asked by hall keepers about a dozen times "Where's your permit?" I said I had none and went on. If I had been on to the ways of the school I would have stuck out any piece of paper and pretended it was a permit. I finally found my room on the third floor of another building, but when I reached it the time alloted for getting to your class room was long since up so I was sent back to my graderoom. By this time I was ready to give up and go home, but I got through the day somehow. On Wednesday and Friday I took swimming (there is a large swimming pool in each building) and the other days we played field hockey when it was fine, or played basket ball and took gym exercises.

When the fiftieth anniversary of Thomas A. Edison's discovery of the Madison Lamp was celebrated, school was let out to see the grand parade, in which were also President Hoover and his wife and Henry Ford. The President and his wife drove along in their limousine behind rows and rows of motor cycles and a car of private detectives, and the same followed. The rain was pouring down, but the top of their limousine was thrown back and the President sat there with his hat off nodding and smiling, and Mrs. Hoover held a bouquet of flowers and was doing the same.

Autobiography of Claire Collins

We made several trips across the St. Clair and Detroit Rivers on the ferry to the Canadian side and also Belle Isle where people from the city go for picnics and parties.

We did not live here long and left for Tennessee right after Christmas (1929) and spent the rest of the holidays with my aunt in Nashville and then came to the little town of Portland where I have now lived for over a year. I like the little town very much. If I ever have any children I want them (unlike myself) to be able to call some certain place in some certain state and country "their home town."

(Claire this is an unusually interesting paper, and it would be quite difficult for me to say how much I've enjoyed it. I feel as if I had almost been to some of those places myself. You have the ability to narrate events in a very entertaining manner, a fact that you should be very proud of. You should indeed feel fortunate in having had such a large store of rich experiences, and I'm sure some of us would be more than willing to swap places with you (if it were possible) and let you have a "home-town.")   M.E.B.

Appendix C

Unequal Yoking
or
"Be Not Unequally Yoked With Unbelievers"

"What Does It Mean?"

Being a treatise on the relationship of the Christian to the world.

By
E. GASTON COLLINS.

INTRODUCTION

I have no apology to make for bringing out a tract, nor any to make for choosing this subject. While many have written on the relationship of the church to the world, I don't remember to have read a tract on this subject. Yet I cannot hope to bring out anything new. This is, in the main, a compilation of scripture references, with some remarks, and quotations from others. The scripture references are from the American Standard Version except as otherwise stated. I hope you may become so interested that you will read them all, and more also.

The position taken herein is the result of some years of study and prayer. I believe in it, it is close to my heart, and it is with an earnest prayer that this may be read and accepted in the same good spirit in which it is written. I have a single desire to do good, to help in building up the church which my Lord died to establish, and to make the world better in the only way in which it will be made better permanently – through the church. "God is light." (1John 1:5) and he gives the light (spiritual blessings) to

Unequal Yoking
by E. Gaston Collins

the world through Christ and his people – "Ye are the light of the world." (Matt. 5:14).

There is the same crying need today, as there has ever been, for a plainer and more marked distinction between the world and God's people. The difference between the Christian and the worldling is not sharp enough. There are too many Christians today who "go down to Egypt (to the world – E.G.C.) for help (and amusement – E.G.C.) and rely on horses and trust in chariots," (Isaiah 31:1) and not enough who wait for Jehovah and trust in him. Many church members are so mixed up with the things of the world that no difference is noticeable. Believing that this difference should be greater and seeing the hurtful effect upon the church of a compromising attitude, I write as I have written.

I use the term "Christian," not in its broad, popular sense, but in the New Testament sense.

The emphasis throughout is mine.

I make no pretentious claim, but I have made an honest effort to arrive at the truth. If I can even in a small measure, increase your interest in Bible reading, your efforts to advance the cause of Christ, or your faith in God who doeth all things well, I shall count my efforts not in vain. With this object in view, and praying God's blessing on you and the tract, I send it forth.

THE AUTHOR

Bridgeport, Ala.,

April 16, 1924.

Appendix C

Be Not Unequally Yoked With Unbelievers. What Does It Mean?

It is commendable for one to seek light. An enquiring, open mind is a progressive mind. Luke says it is noble to "search the scriptures." Acts 17:11. Solomon said, "*Hear instruction,* and be wise and *refuse it not,*" Prov. 8:33. To be open for conviction then is a safe attitude. The "spirit of intelligent criticism thrust from the right place has done incalculable harm," was well said. To refuse "instruction or intelligent criticism" is not a good sign. "To whom was it ever imputed for a fault (by such as were wise) to go over that which he hath done, and to amend it when he saw cause? If we will be sons of the truth, we must consider what it speaketh, and trample upon our own credit, yea, and, upon other men's too, if either be any way an hindrance to it." – Preface to King James Bible. It is proper, right, manly and honest to correct a mistake, but just the opposite to refuse, and leads to the fallacy of infallibility. "Infallibility dethrones reason, puts a stop on investigation and muzzles inquiry. An unreasonable man is always unjust. The man who has no use for reason has no reason to use. By not using his reason he loses it."

The question is, What did Paul, the inspired Apostle, mean, when he said, (2 Cor. 6:14-18) "Be not unequally yoked with unbelievers?" Here is all of the quotation: "Be not unequally yoked with unbelievers; for what fellowship have righteousness and iniquity? or what communion hath light with darkness? and what concord hath Christ with Belial? or what portion hath a believer with an unbeliever? and what agreement hath a temple of God with idols? for we are a temple of the living God; even as God said, I will dwell in them and walk in them, and I will be their God, and they shall be my people. Wherefore come ye out from among them, and be ye separate, saith

Unequal Yoking
by E. Gaston Collins

the Lord, and touch no unclean thing, and I will receive you, and will be to you a father and ye shall be to me sons and daughters, saith the Lord Almighty."

This is a strong statement on the relationship of Christians to the world. He meant what he said, and it is for us to receive it and apply it. If we should properly apply it, it might cost us something, but it would add a great deal of strength and influence to the church, that is spent elsewhere as it is; it would be worth more than all it would cost.

Some say this applies to the marriage question – that a Christian should not marry a non-Christian. Well, it is true that the teaching of the Bible is against mixed marriages. Christians should marry Christians. Sometimes Christians make mistakes when they marry unbelievers, as experience teaches and as many admit. Christian parents should teach their children here. The experience of the Jews in the Old Testament is against mixed marriages. Paul, said, "In honor preferring one another," Rom. 12:10, and if a widow marry let it be, "only in the Lord." 1 Cor. 7:39. Now the first part of the above passage, taken out of its connection, might refer to the marriage question, but I doubt if the passage taken as a whole refers to it, for this reason – Paul, here says, "Come ye out from among them, and be ye separate." But in 1 Cor. 7:8-13, among other things, he says, "that the wife depart not from her husband...and that the husband leave not his wife." The conclusion is clear.

If not marriage, then to what did he refer? Certainly he did not put it in just to fill space – it must mean something. Now read the passage again. It puts righteousness, light, Christ, believers (Christians), and the temple of God, in opposition to iniquity, darkness, Belial,

Appendix C

unbelievers and idols. This is a plain distinction. God and Christ are on one side and the devil on the other. This is the church as opposed to the world. And there is no middle ground between them, no compromise. Further, the passage says, "Come ye out." This indicates that a Christian might for some reason, find himself yoked up with that which is opposed to the church. His duty is clear. Again, that which is opposed to the church or Christ is here pronounced unclean. What is it that cleanses us anyway? "Nothing but the blood of Jesus." When we are cleansed by the blood are we converted? Yes. When converted what body or institution are we a member of? The church. Then nothing but the church was cleansed by the blood. All else is unclean. "Husbands, love your wives, even as Christ also loved the church and gave himself up for it, that he might sanctify it, having cleansed it by the washing of water with the word." Eph. 5:25-26. But if the Christian touches something unclean, seeing his mistake, and comes out of it, God promises to be his father. Wonderful promise. Glorious relationship. Any close fellowship with an unbeliever is forbidden. It is God's will that his worshippers be separate from the world.

A quotation from Bro. David Lipscomb in "Queries and Answers," is here given: "I believe the command covers all relations in which the Christian is controlled by the actions of those not Christians. That is *what yoked together* means – so connected that the actions and course of one not a Christian control the actions of the Christian. This general rule is laid down, then it is pointed out that a neglect of it leads, first to destroy the distinction between righteousness and unrighteousness, then between light and darkness, then it leads into idolatry. The safe ground is to avoid the association that weans from Christ and

Unequal Yoking
by E. Gaston Collins

leads to idolatry. As a precaution against that, the command is, "Be not unequally yoked with unbelievers." We have no formal idolatry, but a great amount of informal idolatry – real idolatry without the forms of idol worship. Whatever a man esteems above service to God is idolatry. Covetousness is idolatry, because a covetous man is more eager to gain money than he is to honor God or to gain his favor. Whatever man holds above service to God is his idol. This scripture tells Christians to avoid the complications and alliances that lead into idolatry. All that weans man from God are embraced. He tells them to come out from among them, from this idol worship, and to withdraw as far as possible from the associations that lead to them. Some associations, like marriage, cannot be broken without violations of other laws of God, and 1 Cor. 7, gives the rules regulating those circumstances.

The devil is the prince of this world. John 14:30, Eph. 2:2. He tried to trade the kingdoms of the world to Christ but failed. Matt. 4:8-9. Christ then and there placed himself in opposition to the world, and his followers should profit by his example. The prophecies concerning the kingdom of Heaven are to the effect that it "shall break in pieces and consume all these kingdoms," (Dan. 2:44), and shall, "dash them in pieces." (Psa. 2:8-9), and they shall "be utterly wasted." Isa. 60:12. And 1 Jno. 5:9 says: "We know that we are of God, and the whole world lieth in the evil one." The devil is opposed to Christ. But many well meaning brethren have made the mistake of working for, and being "yoked" up with, too many worldly things – institutions doing good works, perhaps, but of the world in origin and destiny, nevertheless. Paul says (Rom. 12:2) "And be not fashioned according to this world;" yet many are not worried over the fact that they are so fashioned.

Appendix C

Again (2 Cor. 4:4) "The god (satan) of this world hath blinded the minds of the unbelieving, that the light of the gospel of the glory of Christ, who is the image of God, should not dawn upon them." The devil has many plausible devices by which he blinds men's eyes to the gospel.

Other passages of scripture only strengthen the passage under discussion. A few are herewith submitted:

1. "Pure religion and undefiled ... is this, to visit the fatherless and widows ... and to keep oneself unspotted from the world." Jas. 1:26. Brethren in organizations other than the church justify their membership therin by saying they visit the fatherless and widows. But while keeping the first part of the passage they violate the last part by doing their good in a worldly institution, giving it the glory when "unto him be the glory in the church and in Christ Jesus." (Eph. 3:21) "Will a man rob god?" Mal. 3:8.

2. "Come forth, my people, out of her (Babylon verse 2) that have no fellowship with her sins, and that ye receive not of her plagues," Rev. 18:4.

3. "And have no fellowship with the unfruitful works of darkness, but rather even reprove them," Eph. 5:11. Unfruitful for eternal good. Instead of reproving them, some are associating with and fellowshiping them.

4. "Love not the world, neither the things that are in the world. If any man love the world the love of the father is not in him. For all that is in the world, the lust of the flesh and the lust of the eyes

Unequal Yoking
by E. Gaston Collins

and the vainglory of life, is not of the Father, but is of the world." 1 Jno. 2:15-16.

5. "But ye are a chosen generation, a royal priesthood, an holy nation, a peculiar people: that ye should shew forth the praises of him who hath called you out of darkness into his marvellous light." 1 Pet. 2:9. (a.v.) Did you come all the way out of darkness when you were called? Or have you gone back into things in the dark since you were called? What is there peculiar about your life to distinguish you or whereby you "show forth" his praises? You say baptism and the Lord's Supper weekly. Those are only two of the things that should distinguish you and maybe where you are you can't preach them, and tell your associates that among other things they should be baptized and take the Lord's Supper weekly.

6. "Ye adulteresses, know ye not that the friendship of the world is enmity with God? Whosoever therefore would be a friend of the world maketh himself an enemy of God." Jas. 4:4. How can such a strong passage as this be passed up lightly and not investigated to see what is meant? It means something and somebody may be deceived and be an enemy of God, thinking he is his friend. Spiritual adultery is here meant. The marriage vow to God is broken when we are guilty of what is here termed "friendship of the world."

7. "No man can serve two masters; for either he will hate the one, and love the other, or else he will hold to one, and despise the other. Ye cannot serve God and mammon." Mat. 6:24. Man cannot give his heart to two services at the same time.

Appendix C

This passage helps us explain the carelessness and the falling off of interest in the work of the church, upon the part of church members.

8. "And thou shalt love the Lord thy God with all thy heart and with all thy soul, and with all thy mind, and with all thy strength." Mark 12:30. A demand for supreme love for God. To become affiliated with, and tied up in, things other than the church divides one's strength, and puts our mind, heart and soul, in large measure, as a rule, on these things as can easily be seen. Ruskin correctly said, "There are a great many things which God will put with in a human heart. There is one thing he will not put up with – *a second place.*" Solomon said (Prov. 5:8-10) "Remove thy way far from her, and come not nigh the door of her house, lest thou give thy honor unto others, ... lest *strangers* be filled with thy *strength,* and *thy labors* be in the house of an *alien.*"

9. "Jesus answered, My kingdom is not of this world; if my kingdom were of this world, then would my servants fight, that I should not be delivered to the Jews; but now is my kingdom not from hence." John 18:30. Christ's kingdom is not maintained by carnal weapons, but by spiritual and moral means. If they couldn't consistently fight carnally, to protect him and to uphold his kingdom, how could they do so to uphold another, and a worldly kingdom? If one will practise what Jesus said to do, it will totally unfit him to fight with carnal weapons. A great missionary in South Africa was approached one day by a native in great distress. The native said that his hunting

Unequal Yoking
by E. Gaston Collins

dog had eaten two pages of his Bible, and now he would be useless for the hunt. He argued that because reading the Bible tamed down fierce warriors so that they no longer cared for cruel warfare, it would do the same for a dog. He was right, at least, as to the Bible's transforming effect on men. Men today with no preconceived ideas, and no theories to uphold will get the same idea as the native, if they will faithfully read the New Testament. I read nowhere in the N.T. anything that governs my relationship to a worldly kingdom, save to be submissive to it, and that only when such submission will not cause me to violate some command from God. The Christian is told to pray "for kings" that he may lead a quiet life. That does not mean that I love not my country, but that I love my God more, and owe my allegiance first to him. I appreciate the many blessings enjoyed in this great country, and thank God that by his providence we are so pleasantly situated. But any relationship that will cause a Christian to have to take up carnal weapons and fight in a carnal war to sustain worldly kingdoms is an improper relationship. Any relationship in which a Christian can't serve God in his appointments is an improper relationship. Any relationship that will cause a Christian to think more of non-Christians and less of his brethren in the Lord is an improper relationship. Any relationship in which a Christian is not free to "preach the word" anywhere, or in which he makes no distinction when there is a distinction, or in which he is bound up with those who otherwise make fun of his church and religion,

Appendix C

and call him a "Campbellite," but who tolerate him for the present for his influence, is an improper relationship, and causes him to weaken morally and otherwise in his influence for the church.

10. "For though we walk in the flesh, we do not war according to the flesh (for the weapons of our welfare are not of the flesh, but mighty before God to the casting down of strongholds)" 2 Cor. 10:3-4. The "sword of the spirit" (Eph 6:17) is the Christian's weapon.

11. "No soldier on service *entangleth himself in the affairs of this life,* that he may please him who enrolled him as a soldier." 2 Tim. 2:4. This is a clear, strong statement about the Christian's relationship to the world. It is plainly seen, by the man of faith, who is satisfied with what the Bible says, that "entangling alliances" – "Unequal yokings" – are forbidden. The soldier to do good service, must devote himself entirely to his work. The application is easily made. "Am I a soldier of the cross, a follower of the Lamb" – Jesus Christ, the "Prince of Peace."

12. "For our citizenship (or commonwealth, footnote) is in Heaven; whence also we wait for a saviour ..." Phil. 3:20. Christians are really citizens of Heaven, their country, from which they are now absent, but which they are seeking. Christians are "strangers and pilgrims on the earth, seeking after a country of their own," which will be "a better country, that is a Heavenly" one. (Heb. 11:13-16). Peter writes to us "as sojourners and pilgrims." (1 Pet. 2:11). Brethren, we should set our "mind on

Unequal Yoking
by E. Gaston Collins

the things that are above, not on the things that are upon the earth." (Col. 3:2) It is evident that some things are excluded from "things upon the earth," for Christians are commanded to "work with your hands" and to "provide for his own." But beyond making an honest living, just how far, now, can a Christian go and not "mind earthly things?" (Phil. 3:19.)

13. "But I (Jesus) say unto you, *swear not at all,* neither by the Heaven ... the earth ... Jerusalem ... nor thy head ... But let your speech be Yea, yea, Nay, nay, and whatsoever is more than these is of the evil one." Mat. 5:34-37. James (5:12) repeats this teaching. "*But above all things,* my brethren, *swear not,* neither by the Heaven, nor by the earth, *nor by any other oath,* but let your yea be yea, and your nay, nay; that ye fall not under judgment." This seems to me to forbid all swearing by oaths or vows, and calling upon God to witness it. Desires other than those actuated by the gospel, and the love of Christ, and the love of the church, cause people to reason away the above passages, or explain them differently. But Christians seem to have no hesitancy in "solemnly" asserting, affirming and "sacredly" swearing an "unqualified allegiance" to some earthly government, "above any other and every kind of government in the whole world." That sounds very much like putting some other government ahead of Christ's government. And then, "all to which I have sworn by *this oath* – I will seal with my blood – be thou my witness – Almighty God." (From "the alleged Ku Klux

Appendix C

oath.") Brethren, I must confess to you in all candor, that if this does not constitute an "unequal" *yoking* with a worldly organization, I wouldn't know what would. And it would also be a plain violation of the Saviour's plain command, "Swear not at all."

14. "Every plant which my Heavenly Father planted not, shall be rooted up." Mat. 15:13. "God made man upright; but they have sought out many inventions." Ecc. 7:29. Man's only hope is to hearken to the direction of God and work in that which He has "planted." The good one does through the institutions of men won't bring any blessing from God, and the doer stands a chance to be rooted up with the man-made plant – institution. Human experience goes abundantly to show that it is best to be satisfied with and follow God's plan, rather than to follow the devices of man.

Many other passages teach along the same line – the distinction between the world and the church, but I think these are sufficient. With these plain passages before us it is not a question of what does the Bible say, but what are we going to do – apply them to ourselves and obey God, or ignore them, or reason around them and be popular. The Christian cannot consistently be both obedient to God and popular with the world, at the same time. It has ever been so with God's people. The Saviour says, "many are called but few are chosen," and many enter the broad road, but few the narrow road, and, "They are not of the world, even as I am not of the world," and, "If the world hateth you, ye know that it hath hated me before it hated you. If ye were of the world, the world would love its own, but because ye

Unequal Yoking
by E. Gaston Collins

are not of the world, but I chose you out of the world, therefore the world hateth you." The world always has been, and always will be opposed to the church.

But there are many organizations that require oaths of allegiance. In the light of the scripture there is no reason to believe that the Christian may take any of them.

Someone wants to know why I oppose all these organizations of which many could be named. I wish to be understood as not opposing these organizations only in so far as opposing the membership of Christians in them may be construed as opposing them. These worldly things are all right for the worldly man, if he will understand that when he is converted he is to, "come out from among them." All of these organizations contribute their part to the betterment of conditions in a general way. Paul says, "and we know that to them that love God all things work together for good, even to those that are called according to his purpose." Rom. 8:28. But the Christian has the church, in which to do his good work, and thus give God the glory "in the church" as he has asked us to do. This does not mean that you must conclude, that because one, who is a Christian only, does not oppose what you oppose, in the way you oppose it, he is in favor of everything you oppose. If the worldly man wants to organize to fight what he deems error let him do it. The Christian can't judge such matters. "For what have I to do with judging them that are without? ... But them that are without God judgeth ...." 1 Cor. 5:12-13. The Christian opposes error in God's appointed way. The worldly man can fight in ways in which the Christian cannot. Christians should recognize the fact that there are things they cannot do, in the church. But because of this he should not feel at liberty to join something else in which to do what he could and should

Appendix C

do in the church, and, perhaps, somethings he should not do at all.

Christians believe that the "scriptures thoroughly furnish us unto all good works, that the man of God may be complete." And the man of faith will be content with that. The Christian is complete in the church or Christ. "And he is the head of the body, the church. Who is the beginning, the firstborn from the dead; that in all things he might have the preeminence. For it was the *good pleasure* of the *Father* that *in him* should *all the fulness dwell.* Col. 1:18-19. Christ is "head over all things to the church, which is his body, the fullness of him that filleth all in all." Eph. 1:22-23. Did God purposely or through oversight leave out something he should have said? Or is the New Testament complete and is it meant for, and adapted to, us today? "*Unto Him be the glory in the church and in Christ Jesus unto all generations for ever and ever,* Amen." Eph. 3:21 Certainly, *today* as in Paul's day, Christians are to honor God in the church, and the *same will be true till Jesus comes again.* This world, as distinguished from the church, will never work itself up to that point when it, with all its institutions, will be good enough for the Christian to honor God through. The church shall always be separate from the world, which shall never be a "friend to grace, to help us on to God." Jesus said, "I am with you ... to the end of the world." With those who preach his word. That means those same rules and principles are in force today and shall be, to the end.

Being unequally yoked, divides the Christian's allegiance, time, and means, and frequently causes him to compromise his position, hence weakening his influence in the church. For instance, a professing Christian once asked me, if I didn't think if one was a good Mason he

Unequal Yoking
by E. Gaston Collins

would be saved. Another said the Masonic Lodge has more Bible in it than your church. Another said "The ___ does more good than the church." It is easy to see what such as these are in love with, and that they are usually not very active workers for Christ in the church. Another, who was consistent, said "the ___ lodge is no place for a Campbellite." meaning one who claims to be a Christian only.

Of course, the New Testament being true, salvation is in the church only, which is the same as being in Christ. Salvation is in him. "He is the head of the body, the church." The Christian should not be in anything that weakens his interest in, or influence for the church. He has none to spare. He should not be in anything in which he can't teach and practise the principles of the Christian religion as set forth in the New Testament. And when he is called upon to soft pedal his religion he had better look out.

I have heard it said, "If the church did its duty there would be no use for these other organizations." Of course the ones who say that don't mean to make a confession, but that is a roundabout way of saying they were not doing their duty as Christians. They are just making an excuse; trying to prove an alibi; trying to palliate their conscience. If the charge is true they really say, that when the church is weak these other things are strong. I suppose the reverse would be true – when the church is strong these other things are weak. That's true individually too. When one does his duty as a Christian, and is strong for the church, he has no time or means for other things. But according to the above charge, the church has failed, to some extent at least. While that may be true it is no excuse for the Christian to expend his energies on something else,

Appendix C

then criticize the church. I would like to ask those who make the above charge, if they are sure they have the right standard by which to judge the success of the church. Should the church do what they think it should, and what they are doing in some other way? Really now is the church supposed to control courts and judges and legislators and laws? Is it not rather to "submit to the powers that be" than to control them? If the church succeeded according to their standard, would it be well pleasing to God? When the Israelites wanted to be like the other nations, wanted to be popular, they became weak. When before that, they were as God wanted them to be, although seemingly weak, they were strong. The same has been true with the church.

In Apostolic days, when the church attended to its own affairs, played hands off of everything not its own, even to civil affairs, as even church history, as well as the New Testament, goes abundantly to show, it grew in numbers and spirituality, was strong in the faith and kept the worship pure. But when it began to be popular, and state officials accepted a form of Christianity and began to interfere in church affairs, then it was the church began to weaken. Portions of it became corrupt and factious, and a falling away took place. There began to be a centralized power, out of which grew the two branches of the Catholic Church, and in process of time out of these, and some for other causes, grew the denominations of the present day. Out of this tendency also grew the union of church and state. This was not as it should have been. The church controlled by the state became paralyzed. Or the state controlled by the church became tyrannical. I believe in the separation of church and state, and try to practise it. I think the New Testament teaches it. We should not worry

Unequal Yoking
by E. Gaston Collins

ourselves about *what would happen* if it were practised absolutely by every Christian – no Christian taking any part in affairs of government. That's where the Christian's faith in God plays an important part. I believe conditions would be better were it so. I believe that God would so overrule things as to make it possible for Christian's to "lead a tranquil and quiet life in all godliness and gravity." "God moves in a mysterious way, His wonders to perform." "Surely the wrath of man shall praise thee." I think it near blasphemy, and a sign of little faith, and a source of discontent, for Christians to say that God has nothing to do today in human affairs, by way of overruling them to the good of his children.

The church may be what the world, and some brethren call weak, but if it is doing God's will He will be pleased and will overrule circumstances for the good of the church. "And he hath said unto me, my grace is sufficient for thee, for my power is made perfect in weakness. Most gladly, therefore will I rather glory in my weaknesses, that the power of Christ may rest upon me. Wherefore I take pleasure in weaknesses, in injuries, in necessities, in persecutions, in distresses, for Christ's sake; for when I am weak, then am I strong." 2 Cor. 12:9-10. God has chosen the "foolish, weak, base, despised," things of the world to put to shame the things that seem to be strong, "that no flesh should glory before God."

The world will be made better when the church is made better. Other things may do good, but it is only temporary. It is only a reflected or borrowed goodness. Especially is this true when Christians do their good outside of the church. Anything that does good, if it robs the church and God of the honor that properly belongs to

Appendix C

them only makes matters worse, more complicated, and it becomes harder for people to see the truth.

"Surely the future looks black enough, yet it holds a hope, a single hope. One, and one power only, can arrest the descent and save us. That is the Christian religion. Democracy is but a side issue. The paramount issue is the religion of Christ and Him crucified; the bed rock of civilization; the source and resource of all that is worth having, in the world that is and that gives promise in the world to come, not as an abstraction, but as a mighty force and principle of being. If the world is to be saved from destruction, it will be saved alone by the Christian religion." – Henry Watterson. Brethren, let's give the proper place and estimate to the church ourselves, for if we don't know how can we expect others to do so. Many act as if they had forgotten that God has a church, should be glorified in it, and cannot be glorified in any other institution. Other institutions are doing good. But good works alone will not save. If so, man by his own efforts could save himself – and Christ died in vain. But Paul said, "Work out your own salvation with fear and trembling." Phil. 2:12. We are saved by thus working, "in Christ" – "In whom (Christ) we have our redemption, the forgiveness of our sins." Col. 1:14.

Here is a quotation from Bro. R.H. Boll in the March "Word and Work" under "Christians and the Klan" – Have not the people of God enough light to settle the question of the propriety of joining the "Ku Klux" for themselves? Shall a people who are specially and emphatically warned above all things not to swear (Jas. 5:13) enter into an oath-bound combine? Shall they whom God has set apart for Himself and separated from the world by the triple wall of truth, Spirit, and Blood, enter in to compact and union

Unequal Yoking
by E. Gaston Collins

with non-Christians? (2 Cor. 6:14-18). Shall they who are the beneficiaries of God's world-wide love, who are bound by every high and holy consideration to become all things to all men that by all means they might save some, participate in the drawing of factional lines against their fellow men? Shall they who are solemnly enjoined not to avenge themselves, but to be in subjection to the constituted power and civil authority, take the rightings of wrongs, into their own hands, and assume the exercise of prerogatives to which they have no God-given right? You say, "they do much good!" What sort of "good" is it that is done in contravention to God's plain and specific instructions? Is not obedience better than sacrifice, and to hearken than the fat of rams? I speak not of "them that are without" – I have nothing to do with judging them; God judges their doings. (1 Cor. 5:12-13.) But *you* who wear the name of Christ, who are bound to love and mercy, representatives of the Lord, set apart as saints of God, children of obedience, what have you to do with the masked clan? More even than the sin itself should we fear that fatuous blindness which prevents Christians from seeing it. That, too, is one of the signs."

In the Christian Leader of October 23, 1923, I wrote as follows:

CAN A CHRISTIAN BE A MEMBER OF THE

KU KLUX KLAN?

1. The Klan is a worldly institution. Hence shall be rooted up. Matt. 15:13.

2. Being a worldly institution a Christian can't affiliate with it, since "friendship of the world" is forbidden. James 4:4; 1 John 2:15-17; Col. 2:20-23.

Appendix C

3. Since God is to be glorified in the church (I Peter 4:11, Eph. 3:21), he is not glorified in anything else, by the Christian.

4. Our Lord doesn't take account of every good work. Matt 7:22-23. Hence we should be careful that our good works are properly placed.

5. The Christian needs nothing but the church – Christ. Col. 2:10; 2 Tim. 2:4.

6. Since it is not bought with the blood of the Saviour, it belongs to the world of darkness. And if Christians should be in it, they are commanded to come out. II Cor. 6:14-18; Eph. 5:7-12; I Peter 2:9; Col. 1:13.

7. Loyalty to the Klan will lead its members into war, according to their alleged oath. But war and Christianity are incompatible, according to the Scriptures. John 18:36; 2 Cor. 10:1-5; Rom. 12:19; 2 Tim. 2:24.

8. Christians are solemnly warned to take no oath. Matt. 5:33-37; James 5:12.

Klansmen call God to witness when they seal their oath with their own blood, according to their alleged oath.

Please read the references which I give to save space.

Our "brother in Central Ohio" is to be commended for investigating before joining the Klan. So many do not investigate, but just plunge in, without asking. What does God say about it? *With the Christian, God's Word is final, and the man of faith will follow it.* David Lipscomb said it

Unequal Yoking
by E. Gaston Collins

all depended on what kind of Christian one wanted to be, as to whether or not he joined these worldly institutions,

I do not wish to play the role of an opposer to the Klan so much as I wish to do my whole duty to God, through his divinely ordained plan – the church. The Ku Klux Klan has some good principles, and does some good, doubtless, but if we argue it on that ground, the Catholic Church, which the Klan opposes, would get by. Perhaps the Klan is a good thing for the worldly man, but the line of difference between the world and the church should be drawn plainer than it is.

    Bridgeport, Ala.   E. Gaston Collins

Bishop Candler said at Opelika, Ala., November 14, 1923. the following: "My father lived and died a Mason. I have never found a place for it in my life and habits. I know nothing about it and do not care to criticise it, but I do want to put the ministry on notice that *secret orders do not convert the world*. ..." Bro. Fred M. Little, Montgomery, Ala., says: "I am impressed with this statement as being a hopeful sign that even members of denominations are beginning to realize that fraternal *and religious organizations other than the church hinder rather than aid the preaching of the gospel,* and therefore cannot be encouraged." "Surely the blood bought church is sufficient for all spiritual needs. I am sure the church suffers when members of the one body give encouragement to the support of other religious institutions." He also quotes Bro. John R. Williams, in the Gospel Advocate of November 22, 1923, and I quote him: "Whatever a human institution gives for charitable purposes, that institution gets the glory of it. Brother

Appendix C

Preacher, right here you know you rob Christ of the glory that is his, and give to a human institution the honor and glory that belongs to the institution of Christ." Brother Little further says, "I am not picking dispute with my brother in the church, but I hope we all can find it in our hearts to be content to glorify Christ, through the church." – Christian Leader of March 11, 1924.

"The world knows not Christ, nor does it know his followers." "The followers of Christ were like beings from another world, so it will be with us if ye are Christians. We will be pilgrims, and, of course, strangers here. The world will not understand us. Our motives to action, our joys and hopes, our supports, are all strange to them." "We are bound for another land, and feel strange here. If strangers, let us live so." – Lards Quarterly.

Next I quote Tolbert Fanning in, "The Living Pulpit," Pages 530-531: "Worldly governments are not for the righteous, said Paul; and therefore, God has ordained the men of the world as his ministers to create and direct all institutions worldly. In his spiritual household, our Heavenly Father has reserved the right to govern without the admixture of the least human wisdom, which the Apostle says is 'foolishness with God.' The prince of this world is the head and governor, in all kingdoms and organizations constructed in the wisdom of men. His subjects are such as are devoted to institutions not Divine. Force is the great controlling power.

In Christ's body, on the contrary, the Head is spiritual; his subjects are spiritual; his laws are spiritual, and love is the only motive power. To us these institutions therefore differ across the whole Heavens." ... "In that solemn declaration of the Saviour before Pilate – 'My kingdom is not of this world; if it were, my servants would fight that I

Unequal Yoking
by E. Gaston Collins

should not be delivered to the Jews; but now is my kingdom not from hence-' possibly is embodied all that need be predicated of the spiritual character of the church, for our present purpose. In the Christian institution, then, swords are beaten into plow shares, and spears into pruning hooks, and God's people 'study not war.' No violence was necessary to give success to the government of Christ, and his people employ it not in their journey to the skies. God is their shield and high tower. If, through these great words of the spirit, our friends cannot see the broad line between the church and the world, it is not in my power to describe it."

Ex-President Wilson said, "The sum of the whole matter is this, that our civilization cannot survive materially unless it be redeemed spiritually. It can be saved only by becoming permeated with the spirit of Christ and being made free and happy by the practices which spring out of that spirit. Only thus can discontent be driven out and all the shadows lifted from the road ahead."

Men may differ as to the method of attaining this much needed condition, but the ex-President, at least, had the right idea, and he learned it from the Bible and experience. So I say to Christians, let's busy ourselves in spreading the gospel of our Lord, and getting people to accept it and drink in the spirit of Christ. Let's lay our all on the altar of service to God. Let's say what Moses said in the long ago to Pharaoh, when the latter tried to get him to compromise in his attitude toward God. "There shall not a hoof be left behind." Ex. 10:26. Let us say as does the song, "All to Jesus I surrender, all to Him I freely give." "Jesus paid it all, all to him I owe." Why should it be otherwise? Frances R. Havergal very beautifully said, in substance, "Take my life, hands, feet, voice, lips, silver and

Appendix C

gold, ("not a mite would I withhold") moments, intellect, will, heart, love, myself and consecrate it, Lord, to Thee; let it be ever, only, all for Thee." She learned that from the Bible. Paul said, "How be it what things were gain to me, these have I counted loss for Christ. Yea verily and I count all things to be loss for the excellency of the knowledge of Christ Jesus my Lord, for whom I suffered the loss of all things and do count them but refuse, that I may gain Christ." Phil. 3:7-8. "But I hold not my life of any account as dear unto myself ..." Acts 20:24. If the majority of people were Christians and the church was going forward by leaps and bounds, Christians would have a better excuse, yet no reason, for dividing their time and means with other things, but, much as we dislike to own it, "there remaineth yet very much land to be possessed."

The Christian should first, last and all the time be for the church. He should consecrate to her all his "beings ransomed powers." He should rejoice in every success of the gospel, and pray and work for its spread. So I plead with my brethren to give the church a square deal – to put it first – to give God a chance in their lives. I plead for them to so live that, "When we are judged ... we may not be condemned with the world." This can be done best by coming "out from among them," and being the "separate" people that God teaches we should be.

"Search the Scriptures!"

Appendix D

Does it Pay to Go to Church?
by E. Gaston Collins
(handout for the Radnor Church of Christ)

Have you ever asked yourself the question, "What can I do to make this world a better dwelling place?" And why shouldn't everyone *want* to do something worthwhile, and helpful? Why be aimless and drifting? There is so much to do that it is a crime to neglect life's opportunities. Being weak and limited in ability is not failure, but to try no longer, to have no aim or a low, mean, selfish aim is failure.

But what can Radnor Christians do?

From the "Declaration of Principles," by the American Prison Association, I quote, "Of all reformatory agencies, *Religion* is the *first* in importance, because it is most potent in its actions upon the heart and life."

Judge Lewis L. Fawcett, of the Supreme Court of New York State, is a veteran on the bench. He has sentenced over 8,000 persons convicted of crime, and he said that of that number, very few were members of or attendants at any church or Sunday school. An 18-year old youth convicted of murders, said to him, "My downfall commenced when I stopped going to Sunday school." Many others say the same thing.

The Judge says that the churches and her ministers can aid greatly in helping those guilty of crime. He said, "In 1,092 cases of suspended sentences, in each of which a minister became interested at my request, only 62 boys ever came back for violating their parole." He thinks the others reformed permanently, and that there is some hope

Does it Pay to Go to Church
by E. Gaston Collins

for a future life of usefulness for a boy if he will go to church and Sunday school.

The Judge further says:

"When Sunday school attendance increases, crime decreases ...

"No child can have a fair American chance without religion ...

"Crime would cost many times more if the churches were closed ...

"I regard our Sunday schools and churches as the only effective means to stem the rising tide of vice and crime among youth ...

"If every Christian would do his duty we could capture the youth of America for Jesus Christ in one generation and practically put an end to crime."

Moral – Go to church; worship God; serve Jesus Christ by helping mankind, and living "soberly, righteously, and godly in this present world," for it pays big morally, spiritually, and materially to do so.

Appendix E

List of Songs from "Song Hints" by E. Gaston Collins in *Around the Lord'sTable* Gospel Advocate Company, 1934.

- "Man of Sorrows," What a Name!
- Holy, Holy, Holy, Lord God Almighty!
- O Worship the King All-Glorious Above
- In the Hour of Trial, Jesus, Plead for Me
- I Need Thee Ev'ry Hour
- Majestic Sweetness Sits Enthroned
- O for a Thousand Tongues to Sing
- Tell me the Story of Jesus
- In the Cross of Christ I Glory
- King of My Life, I Crown Thee Now
- My Life, My Love, I Give to Thee
- There Comes to My Heart One Sweet Strain
- I Will Sing the Wondrous Story
- The Great Physician Now is Near
- O Day of Rest and Gladness
- Safely through Another Week
- Blest Feast of Love Divine
- The King of Heav'n His Table Spreads
- Amidst Us Our Beloved Stands
- Welcome, Sweet Day of Rest
- In Memory of the Saviour's Love
- I Stand Amazed in the Presence
- Again the Lord of Light and Life
- Another Week with All Its Cares Hath Flown
- Bread of the World
- Break Thou the Bread of Life

List of Songs from "Song Hints" by E. Gaston Collins

- By Christ Redeemed
- Why Did My Saviour Come to Earth?
- I Feed My Faith on Christ
- Jesus Invites His Saints
- Jesus Thou Joy of Living
- A Parting Hymn We Sing
- Till He Come
- From Calvary a Cry Was Heard
- Jesus Keep Me Near the Cross
- Nearer the Cross
- Night with Ebon Pinion
- There is a Fountain Filled with Blood
- On a Hill Far Away Stood an Old Rugged Cross
- Thy Life Was Given for Me
- 'Tis Midnight and on Olive's Brow
- When I Survey the Wondrous Cross
- When My Love to Christ Grows Weak
- Alas! and Did My Saviour Bleed?
- From Every Stormy Wind That Blows
- Guide Me O Thou Great Jehovah
- I Hear the Savior Say
- Nearer, Still Nearer
- O Love That Will Not Let Me Go
- Rock of Ages, Cleft for Me
- Savior, Thy Dying Love
- There Is a Green Hill Far Away
- There Was One Who Was Willing to Die in My Stead
- On the Holy Lord's Day Morning
- That Dreadful Night Before His Death
- Here, O My Lord, I See Thee Face to Face

Appendix E

- Lord, at Thy Table We Behold
- Dark Was the Night, and Cold the Ground
- Jesus Wept! Those Tears Are Over
- Bread of Heaven
- Blest Feast Divine
- From the Table Now Retiring
- Jesus, Lover of My Soul
- Upon the First Day of the Week
- My Jesus, I Love Thee
- Savior, More Than Life to Me
- On the Cross of Calvary
- I Gave My Life for Thee
- Lord, We Come Before Thee Now
- I Love Thy Kingdom Lord
- I Hear Thy Welcome Voice
- How Pleasing to Behold and See
- Lord, I Hear of Showers of Blessing
- Christ, Our Redeemer, Died on the Cross
- On Calv'ry's Brow My Savior Died
- There is No Love Like the Love of Jesus
- Love Divine, All Love Excelling

Appendix F

TO READ THE ENTIRE BIBLE IN TWELVE MONTHS

―――o―――

"If God is a reality, and the soul is a reality, and you are an immortal being, what are you doing with your Bible shut?"—JOHNSON.

―――o―――

"This Book will keep me from sin;
Or sin will keep me from this Book."

Published By
E. GASTON COLLINS
1701 Green Hills Drive
Nashville (4) Tenn.

―――o―――

with the
Algood, Huntland, and Ashland City, Tenn., Churches
Co-operating.

―――o―――

AUGUST, 1943

To Read The Entire Bible In Twelve Months
by E. Gaston Collins

TO READ THE ENTIRE BIBLE IN TWELVE MONTHS

By E. Gaston Collins

"Save for my daily range among the pleasant fields of Holy Writ, I might despair."—*Alfred, Lord Tennyson.*

There are a number of outlines to aid one in reading the Bible through in a given time. Some years ago there fell into my hands this simple, workable arrangement, by D. F. Merritt, minister, of Dorsett, Vt. He wrote, "For a long time I have read the Bible through every year according to this schedule; I begin the month reading five chapters a day which allows for days when I am not able to read at all, and for miscellaneous reading the latter part of the month."

But it is safer to be a faithful daily reader, for it is dangerous and amazingly easy to become so busy no time is left for Bible reading. We should make it our sacred daily business.

In addition to other Bible study I have without fail read it through yearly, for nineteen years now, following this schedule. A notation on page 1 of the text, in a cherished old Bible, the gift of two friends, says, "Began reading through on January 1, 1924," and at the end of Revelation, it says, "Finished entire Bible December 31, 1924." That was the beginning; each year since it has been repeated.

It is a big help to have this monthly schedule, and it may be changed to meet differing circumstances. I find a good program for ministers is to read an average of four chapters each week-day, and none on this schedule on Sundays. Others may read a lesser number on week-days and more on Sundays.

On each yearly excursion the Bible will mean more and more to you. An extra dividend may be yours by keeping a note-book handy in which to enter impressive thoughts, or references on various Bible topics.

To some, reading the entire Bible, page after page, within a given time, might seem to be an insurmountable task, taking more time than one has. From this schedule one can readily see that it is not such a task. If one loves the Word of God as he should (2 Thess. 2:10), he will find time for reading it, and relish it, for his spiritual development.

A simple calculation: suppose one reads eight hours a day, an ordinary working day, for nine days, less than a two weeks vacation, he could easily read once through the entire Bible on this schedule, and have time left for relaxation during his vacation. How this procedure would improve some vacations! But this systematic plan gives one an entire year.

From every viewpoint the Bible is the greatest Book of all. It has been translated, in whole or in part, into more than 1,000 languages and dialects, far more than any other book. Its influence is immeasurable; it is

Appendix F

not just *a* book—it is pre-eminently *the* Book. It retains the lead each year as "the best seller." Yet to many it is a closed Book—they cannot understand it because they do not read it, not to mention study! Such neglect cheats many out of God's blessing. (Rev. 1:3.) It is a revelation from God to man; man cannot know God without knowing the Bible; verily, man cannot know himself in the right light without knowing the Bible. This amazing Book is the only bridge across a deep chasm, for there is no other way to a knowledge of the one true God. And no matter what its enemies say the old bridge is still safe, for it has been tried by thousands who have crossed and are now crossing over on it.

Kind Reader, won't you give it a chance? And yourself a chance? And God? Start now on your yearly Bible tour; you have nothing to lose, and everything worthwhile to gain. You may make sure of heaven by so doing, for you need Bible power on the journey. (Rom. 1:16.)

> "He cannot fail for He is God;
> He cannot fail, He pledged His word;
> He cannot fail, He'll see me through,
> 'Tis God with whom I have to do."—Sel.

In the words of another:

"This book contains the mind of God, the state of man, the doom of sinners, the happiness of believers. Its doctrines are holy, its precepts are binding, its histories are true, and its decisions are immutable. Read it to be wise, believe in it to be safe, and practice it to be holy. It contains light to direct you, food to support you, and comfort to cheer you. It is the traveler's map, the pilgrim's staff, the pilot's compass, the soldier's sword, and the Christian's charter.

"Here Paradise is restored, heaven opened, and the gates of hell disclosed. Christ is its grand object, our good its one design, and the glory of God its end. It should fill the memory, rule the heart, and guide the feet. Read it slowly, repeatedly and prayerfully. It is a mine of wealth, a paradise of glory, and a river of pleasure. It is given you in life, will be opened in the judgment, and will be remembered forever. It involves the highest responsibility, will reward the greatest labor, and will condemn all who trifle with its sacred contents."

(During a yearly reading not long since, I timed myself, at a reasonable rate; so, I add the "Reading Time" feature to the following schedule to encourage regular Bible reading. "Try it, you can succeed.")

	Chap.	Reading Time		
		Hr.	Min.	Sec.
JANUARY				
Genesis	50	3	22	
Exodus	40	2	40	30
Matthew	28	1	54	30
FEBRUARY				
Leviticus	27	2	4	
Numbers	36	2	42	
Mark	16	1	16	45
MARCH				
Deuteronomy	34	2	29	
Joshua	24	1	38	
Judges	21	1	36	15
Luke	24	2	11	

To Read The Entire Bible In Twelve Months
by E. Gaston Collins

	Chap.	Reading Time		
		Hr.	Min.	Sec.
APRIL				
Ruth	4		12	30
I Samuel	31	2	5	30
II Samuel	24	1	46	
I Kings	22	2	2	
John	21	1	34	10
MAY				
II Kings	25	1	53	45
I Chronicles	29	2	1	30
II Chronicles	36	2	18	40
Acts	28	2	5	5
JUNE				
Ezra	10		39	15
Nehemiah	13	1	1	25
Esther	10		29	45
Job	42	1	42	10
Romans	16		47	
JULY				
Psalms	89	(See August Total)		
I Corinthians	16		48	55
AUGUST				
Psalms	61	4	11	35
Proverbs	31	1	31	35
II Corinthians	13		34	
SEPTEMBER				
Ecclesiastes	12		30	30
Song of Solomon	8		15	5
Isaiah	66	3	36	10
Galatians	6		16	40
Ephesians	6		15	40
OCTOBER				
Jeremiah	52	3	58	50
Lamentations	5		20	35
Philippians	4		12	
Colossians	4		11	30
I Thessalonians	5		8	45
II Thessalonians	3		5	30
I Timothy	6		12	
II Timothy	4		9	
Titus	3		8	45
Philemon	1		2	30
NOVEMBER				
Ezekiel	48	3	14	15
Daniel	12		60	15
Hosea	14		29	30
Joel	3		11	15
Hebrews	13		36	15
James	5		14	45
DECEMBER				
Amos	9		23	15
Obadiah	1		3	
Jonah	4		7	45
Micah	7		18	
Nahum	3		7	30
Habakkuk	3		11	
Zephaniah	3		9	15
Haggai	2		5	30
Zechariah	14		32	15
Malachi	4		9	
I Peter	5		13	
II Peter	3		7	45
I John	5		11	30
II John	1		1	15
III John	1		1	20
Jude	1		3	15
Revelation	22		57	15
OLD TESTAMENT	929	54	10	20
NEW TESTAMENT	260	15	20	5
BIBLE (66 BOOKS)	1189	69	30	25

Appendix G

Who Were the "Very Chiefest Apostles"?
by E. Gaston Collins
(*Word and Work* magazine, April 1955, pp. 78-80)

Not many months back it was my genuine pleasure to be in the company of three well known and highly esteemed brethren, whom I love. All of us are preachers of many years experience, possibly totaling close to two hundred years for the four of us. That represents a vast amount of Bible study, and much communion with God. Our conversation was all pleasant and elevating, and, with many happy reminiscenses, we naturally included some Bible questions. But being the youngest of the group, like Elihu, I thought, "Days should speak, and the multitude of years should teach wisdom." Yet, I ventured the question, "WHO WERE THE 'VERY CHIEFEST APOSTLES' THAT PAUL REFERRED TO"? In short order the three brethren answered, "the twelve apostles." While I attempted to explain why I didn't think so, I didn't get very far with it – other things came up, we passed on, and I didn't insist.

The three brethren's answer doubtless represents the thinking of many others, as I have observed. Bur for a long time I have not thought the above answer correct. So I here state why, and it should also be of general interest, and promote helpful thinking.

Please refer to 2 Corinthians chapters 10, 11, 12, for the full context. Observe that Paul begins ch. 11 with, "Would that ye could bear with me in a little foolishness." False teachers had disparaged his claims, which, with the attitude of some of his brethren at Corinth, compelled a self-defense. One as humble and consecrated as Paul could only do this with some sense of shame. So he apologizes for it. His word "foolishness" is repeated in vs.

Who Were the 'Very Chiefest Apostles'?
by E. Gaston Collins

17 and 21; and the word "foolish" is used some five or more times here. These words literally haunt these chapters. They "compelled" him to say, "seeing that many glory after the flesh, I will glory also," (11:18) i.e. pardon this "foolishness." The false teachers claimed to be apostles, and were belittling Paul's work and claims, so he writes sarcastically. Hence, to say that Paul refers to the twelve apostles of Christ, when he says "the very chiefest apostles," is to miss his point altogether. It would also be to cast Paul in a role foreign to his true character – off-color for him – for he was not one for boasting (this word being used many times in these chapters). He speaks kindly in the highest terms when he refers to "all the apostles," i.e., the twelve. He says he was "the child untimely born," and adds, "For I am the least of the apostles, that am not meet to be called an apostle, because I persecuted the church of God," (I Cor. 15:8,9). This great and humble man of God spoke here without sarcasm, far different from when he referred to "those preeminent apostles." His humility extended further than that, when he said, "Unto me, who am less than the least of all saints." (Eph. 3:8) Again speaking very humbly he calls himself the chief of sinners. How unfair then is it to picture Paul "without understanding," (10-12) in seriously "comparing" himself with the twelve? In that light his irony can be understood, for *the twelve were not giving him any trouble* at Corinth, or anywhere else.

His effort in these three chapters was to expose those he calls "false apostles, deceitful workers, fashioning themselves into apostles of Christ," hence, to say he refers to the twelve apostles when he says, "the very chiefest apostles," is completely out of line with his line of thought. He is trying also to show the church how foolish it was for

Appendix G

any Christian at Corinth to "bear with the foolish gladly, being wise unto yourselves," – scathing irony. (Cp. I Cor. 1:10)

Furthermore, what point could be served in Paul's bringing up at this date an unwholesome comparison between himself and the twelve, and thus continuing that old feeling of strife, when the twelve were not his competitors at Corinth? Perhaps he never had to contend with that old temptation to seek position, as the twelve were troubled – "who then is the greatest?" and, asking for the right hand and the left hand in the kingdom. Doubtless even the twelve had been "converted" on that point by this date. Rather, as between himself and other bona-fide servants of God, he was content to let the work speak for itself; as we often say "eternity alone" can reveal the good one does. Hence, the utter distaste Paul displays in the strong words he uses here in speaking of himself and his detractors. He gave them the simple truth when they forced him to it. If he sought self-vindication it was not between himself and the twelve. The Lord deliver us from that unwarranted conclusion.

Commentators generally agree with the position I have presented, including Brother McGarvey (as I remember). I recently consulted A.T. Robertson's "WORD PICTURES IN THE NEW TESTAMENT." The following quotations from him, if lengthy, are clear and enlightening. He says:

On 11:5 and 12:11, "The rare compound adverb huperlian (possibly used in the vernacular) is probably ironical also, 'the super apostles' as these Judaizers set themselves up to be. 'The extra-super apostles', (Farrar). He is not referring to the pillar-apostles of Gal. 2:9." It seems also that ch. 11:13 would sustain this position too –

Who Were the 'Very Chiefest Apostles'?
by E. Gaston Collins

for such men are false apostles, deceitful workers, fashioning themselves into apostles of Christ."

On ch. 12:11 he further says, I am become foolish ... "In spite of what he said in v.6, that he would not be foolish if he gloried in the other Paul. But it seems that he has dropped back to the mood of 11:1,16. ...He literally means, 'I ought now to be commended by you' instead of having to glorify myself. He repeats his boast already made (11:51), that he is no whit behind 'the super-extra apostles'. Even boasting himself against those false apostles causes a reaction of feeling that he has to express (cf. I Cor. 15:9; Ti. 1:15f.)."

Further, on ch. 11:13 he says, "Masquerading as apostles of Christ by putting on the outward habiliments, posing as ministers of Christ ('gentlemen of the cloth', nothing but cloth). Paul plays with this verb in vs. 13, 14, 15." ("Fashioning," "fashioneth," "fashion.")

On v.14, "The prince of darkness puts on the garb of light and sets the fashion for his followers in the masquerade to deceive the saints. 'Like master like man!' cf. 2:11 and Ga. 1:8. This terrible portrayal reveals the depth of Paul's feelings about the conduct of the Judaizing leaders in Corinth. In Ga. 2:4 he terms those in Jerusalem 'false brethren.'"

On v.15, "Jesus (John 10:1-21) terms these false shepherds thieves and robbers. It is a tragedy to see men in the livery of heaven serve the devil."

On v.16, "Paul feels compelled to boast of his career and work as an apostle of Christ after the terrible picture just drawn of the Judaizers. He feels greatly embarrassed in doing it. Some men can do it with complete composure (sang froid)."

Appendix G

On v.23, As one beside himself ... "beside one's wits. Only here in the New Testament. Such open boasting is out of accord with Paul's spirit and habit ... He claims superiority now to these 'super-extra apostles.'"

-- Borden, Indiana.

Appendix H

Hot A-Plenty By Now
(Or, A Rather Rude Disillusionment)
by E. Gaston Collins

This is an account of a hitherto unreported, interesting incident in the history of a most tragic condition in a brotherhood that *preaches peace* and appeals for unity, but *practices partisanism* (in the name of loyalty and soundness). I believe this was a pivotal incident, presenting a golden opportunity to a man of whom it might have been said, that he came to his position for just "such a time as this." But he allowed it to pass. "Of all sad words of tongue or pen, the saddest are these, 'It might have been.'" If, and when, history completes the record, the story I relate here, should, in all fairness, be included. Bear with me if I (necessarily) include some personal references. And any references to others are also necessary, and given as kindly as I know how, and with no reflection intended, for I try to give them credit for doing what they did conscientiously; believe them to have been mistaken at some points.

There are dozens and scores of similar incidents, yet "off the record," which, if told would fill volumes – many of these in my own experiences portraying the unbrotherly tactics followed, mostly by preachers professing to follow the meek and lowly One, who prayed that "they all might be one."

To get on with the story, it will be necessary to include a few events in connection with my work with the Gospel Advocate here in Nashville, where I worked almost exactly six years. About the first of September, 1931, when I had been preaching nearly two years for the good church at Portland, Tennessee, during the big tent meeting (as

Hot A-Plenty by Now
by E. Gaston Collins

Portland used to have them), conducted that year by B.C. Goodpasture, then of Atlanta, Foy E. Wallace, Jr., came to Portland one day to interview me about working in the Advocate office. This was altogether *unexpected* on my part. Foy had been made editor of the Advocate only a few weeks prior to this time, and from published statements of his, and general expectations, every one was looking for a "*new deal*" on the old paper. In his interview Foy appeared rather uncreedalistic, not asking many questions, not sounding out my "soundness", then. One remark is clear in my mind: he said, "I suppose you are familiar with the policy of the Advocate?" I thought I was -- had been reading it for years. It was a comparatively brief interview, for such a step as this. He invited me to consider the matter, and asked me to come for a visit in the office. This I did, and after thinking it over for a few days, decided to take the place as "office secretary" and editor of the news reports.

We moved later in September to Beechwood Avenue, in Nashville. Almost immediately I was asked to lead the singing in a meeting at Waverly-Belmont church, within a block of our residence. The meeting began on September 27, 1931, with that elegant Christian gentleman, the late Clarence Wilkerson doing the preaching. (I preached for at least two years for W.B. following this.)

On the following Monday night, September 28 Brother Robert H. Boll came to the meeting as he passed through the city from a meeting in Mt. Pleasant, Tennessee. He sat on the back seat of the amen corner at my right. Brethren Foy Wallace and S.H. Hall were present also and sat on the front seat of the same amen corner. Well, for some

Appendix H

unknown reason to me (doubtless a kind, over-ruling providence), I spoke to two of the three elders of the Waverly-Belmont church, saying, "Brother Boll of Louisville is here tonight; how about calling on him for prayer?" Both agreed to it, (and I didn't argue it or persuade). When the time came for prayer I called on him, and he responded.

After dismissal that night, what appears now, in perspective, to be a very strange thing, took place. Foy and Hall were the first to reach me, and *both ardently congratulated* me on havinfg the "courage" to call on Brother Boll. Tho' to me it was an abiding sense of Christian fairness that moved me. I deeply appreciated their encouragement, and as we three stood there shaking hands, I was thinking, perhaps there is some thing to the hoped-for "new deal" – maybe a new day is coming, a day of better feeling among brethren. Maybe Foy and Hall also felt as I did, honestly hoping for a restored fellowship with one less faction to embarrass us.

My amazement rose to new heights the next morning, Tuesday. Foy arrived at the office about 9:00 a.m. As soon as he came in he referred to the night before and said, "Write out a report on Brother Boll passing through town, and of his meeting and *run it in the paper.*" Bolstering his order to run the report, Foy added this *significant statement,* "I'm NOT ALL HET UP ON THE BOLL MATTER." (Foy, do you remember saying that? I will remember it as long as I live.)

Accordingly I prepared the following report: "R.H. Boll, Louisville, Kentucky, called on us and reports an interesting meeting at Mt. Pleasant, Tennessee, with 24

Hot A-Plenty by Now
by E. Gaston Collins

baptisms and three restorations. He closed last Sunday night."

That 4-line report appears on page 1236, bound volume of the Gospel Advocate for 1931, date of October 1st. Look it up and see. Brethren, "BELIEVE IT OR NOT," that was on the order of Foy E. Wallace, Jr., erstwhile editor of the Gospel Advocate, supposed bringer of a "new deal," not then "*all het up on the Boll matter.*"

Here's another interesting observation – that report is found in a group of three, one from Foy himself who had been in a meeting at McMinnville, Tennessee, and one from F.B. Srygley – no collusion, purely co-incidental. This suggestion by Foy to report Brother Boll's meeting was altogether voluntary on his part. All I did was agree.

No ill effects were felt the first week of the meeting, no anathemas were hurled at us. But the calm was soon to be broken, and my new hope was short-lived – sadly it died, almost at birth. Perhaps I expected too much too soon. Apparently the hatchet is not so quickly and easily buried. My anxious hope grew out of a sincere desire to see another rupture in our brotherhood averted, rather I should say another rupture healed.

The second Monday night of the meeting, October 5th Brother F.B. Srygley, who had returned from a meeting of his own, was present at our meeting and in the same amen corner. I believe I called on him for prayer that night. BUT immediately following dismissal, the scene was changed. Instead of congratulating me as the other two brethren had, Brother Srygley took me rather severely to task for calling on Brother Boll for prayer. I said, "But Brother

Appendix H

Srygley, he led a good prayer." He said, "But what did you want to do it for?" I said, "Well, I asked the elders and it was all right with them." He was very emphatic that I shouldn't have called on Brother Boll for prayer.

As I look back from here to that date, 24 years ago I regard that as the *turning point* in Foy's attitude "on the Boll matter." While he and I enjoyed one sweet week there of freedom in the matter, it was not long after that second Monday night of our meeting till Foy became ignited and was soon all aflame "on the Boll matter," Much of what has followed is well-known history. Many unbrotherly and unwarranted charges have been made, and the lines of disfellowship have been forced upon us and rigidly drawn, which I believe to be contrary to both the spirit and the letter of the New Testament. From the above it would appear rather clear who supplied the spark that led to Foy's becoming "all het up on the Boll matter." Entrenched traditions are not abandoned so readily – faces must be saved. If Foy has been called a quick-change artist because of his changing on other matters, such as the war question, how much more is he to be known because of his sudden change "on the Boll matter?" And this change was made months before his change on the war question.

It was not many weeks after the above incident till Foy became so "het up on the Boll Matter" that he began to rate me as undesirable, and he relieved me of the work of editing the news reports and gave it to another. This was only a forerunner, for he tried his best, in one way or another, to remove me from the Advocate office altogether. I was told that two men were slated, by him, at different times, to take my place in the office. (As you'll

Hot A-Plenty by Now
by E. Gaston Collins

see, this did not materialize.) I had a letter from one of the two men about the matter. Failing in one way to remove me, he even tried to get me to say I'd take a church as regular minister, and he even offered to find the location for me, away from Nashville, of course, even tho' I was not "sound" enough to work on the Advocate. But Leon McQuiddy, the owner, said no – "Collins, I don't plan to fire you; *you can stay on as long as you want to.*" Under peculiar circumstances Brother Leon remained my friend to his last day (and I loved him for it, and bless his memory). I did remain there until in 1937, I left voluntarily when we moved to the good church at Lawrenceburg, Tennessee, possibly two years after Foy had been *forced to leave the Advocate.*

Many admirers have regarded him as a courageous man; they counted on him to stand *unflinching* and *flat-footed* for what he believed in – in a *"they-shall-not-pass"* manner, as he often said in those days. As an illustration of this another incident comes to mind. One morning several brethren were visiting in the office; as we stood there talking, Foy arrived. One of them, Will Totty, said, "Foy, I hear you are going to preach on the second coming?" The Editor's reply was, "*I will if I want to,*" just like that, with a typical bang of his fist on the book counter. Well, all but one of us, thought that was something, revealing a man who could and would stand for his convictions. While these incidents show that at one time he was "not all het up on the Boll matter," for he said so himself, time and events show clearly that *he couldn't stand the pressure* in this case, and *he folded and gave way before the entrenched, popular requirements that pass for soundness. So, just how courageous was he?*

Appendix H

Why didn't he courageously stand by and defend and contend for his beliefs then? Oh, how I have wished many times since that he had. We can only imagine what the story might have been had he done so. What a *golden opportunity he muffed!* Was he right then? Did he manifest the right spirit when he congratulated me and ordered me to run Brother Boll's report in the paper? If Foy can answer Foy I'm sure it would be interesting and revealing.

I realize a man may change his mind, and perhaps on occasion he should, to be wise. I've heard it said, "A wise man changes his mind; a fool never." But that would all depend. I do not think his change in this case was wise, when he changed from an attempt to find freedom and to practice fairness, to a state of *bondage under tradition.*

> Do you remember the classic lines?
> "There is a tide in the affairs of men.
> Which, taken at the flood, leads on to fortune;
> Omitted, all the voyage of their life
> Is bound in shallows and in miseries."

Borden, Indiana
March 5, 1955

Appendix I

Memos
on
The Collins Cemetery Association
(by E. Gaston Collins)

This family historic cemetery is located about one and a half miles northeast of the town of Huntland, Tenn., just off the Collins Lane, on the farm owned at one time by W.L. Collins, my grandfather. It is now owned by a Mr. Ballard and operated by his son, Raymond Ballard.

The word "association" is used here, not in a legal sense, but simply referring to friends and descendants of our family, and of several other forebearers now resting in the old cemetery.

Until his decease Uncle Joe Collins assumed practically the entire care of the cemetery. After that Aunt Mary Collins (Mrs. J.N. Smith) deeded the cemetery plot, and a right-of-way to it, to three trustees, Buford Keith, Sr., Knox Moore, Jr., and myself. Upon the death of Buford, his son Buford, Jr., was appointed to and accepted the place of his father. (See papers showing this and related matters.)

We asked Cousin Lexie Moore Bonner, of Huntland, to act as our Secretary-Treasurer. She kindly accepted the appointment, and disbursed the funds faithfully as long as she felt physically able to do so. She then passed this responsibility back to me, along with the balance of funds on had, plus a contribution of her own and an amiable contribution from Cousin Maymie Moore Renegar. I accepted this work temporarily, hoping to find an interested younger party to do this for us. I have succeeded in adding to the fund, as reported below. See

Collins Cemetery Association
by E. Gaston Collins

also First American National Bank, savings book, where the funds are on deposit.

Some of us contributed funds and a good, heavy wire fence was purchased. To this fund Cousin Horace N. Mann (Hohenwald) gave $50.00. Ratio Moore and his friend Mr. Montoy, both of Huntland, erected the fence without charge.

The following also have helped in cleaning off the cemetery: my son-in-law, Griffin Cook, and two sons, David and Billy, Lewisburg, Tenn. Also they have furnished transportation to Huntland on business for the cemetery. My nephew, Collins Steensland and two sons, Eric and Billy, of Nashville have helped in cleaning it off. Jeff C. Moore of Winchester has also furnished me transportation.

Oran Walker, of Huntland, has been helpful. He suggested Woodrow Wiseman (Col.) to clean off the cemetery, and Oran passed on to him funds from me in payment for his work.

In addition to the above funds for the cemetery, and perhaps others not known to me, I have received the following:

Mrs. Willie Steensland	$5.00
Mrs. Tulliah Mann Smith	2.00
Mrs. Arthur (Arie Mann) Cole	5.00
Collins E. Steensland	5.00
Wilma (Mrs. E.J.) Spicer	2.50
Verna Collins	2.50
Lexie Bonner	10.00
Lexie Bonner, Bd.	9.80
Maymie Renegar	*25.00
total	$66.80

Appendix I

On January 18, 1965 I sent a check to Oran Walker, for Woodrow Wiseman, for cleaning; 2 days. $12.00

Balance as of 2-23-65 $55.16

Mr. Fred Ralston (funeral director, Fayetteville Tenn.) contributed $10.00 April 26, 1965 to the cemetery fund. Also his, Mrs. Douglas Binns, Nashville, Tenn. contributed $25.00 on April 26, 1965. On January 4, 1966, daughter Verna $2.50. On January 4, 1966, daughter Wilma, $2.50.

During 1965 my daughter Claire (Mrs. Griffin Cook, Lewisburg, Tennessee) and her son David (Nashville) took me several times to Huntland, Tenn., and the cemetery. Her daughter Jane drove Sunday p.m., Oct. 31, 1965, to the cemetery. On one such trip son Frank Cook made a list of those buried there, whose names were marked. (See attached list.) On Nov. 20, Houston D. Williams drove Griffin Cook's truck, and I and Frank went to the cemetery, and all helping him some as we cleaned off the cemetery. On all these trips Griffin made no charge for use of his truck or car. Neither did David.

On these and numerous other trips to the cemetery, I have gladly contributed freely of my time and services. On nearly all these visits we had difficulty in getting up through the right-of-way; at times it was almost completely blocked, with old farm implements, school buses, and loads of gravel. On one visit to the cemetery we found a large hole in the heavy wire fence through which the cows had had free access to the cemetery.

On January 8, 1966, I wrote a letter to each of the other two trustees, asking for assistance in looking after the cemetery and proposing to remove several large cedar

Collins Cemetery Association
by E. Gaston Collins

trees from the cemetery and sell the logs, funds from which to be used in cost of upkeep. But to this date, March 13, 1966 I have no reply.

The following is a list of names of those buried in the Collins Cemetery, including dates of birth and death as best we could determine. The list was prepared by Frank N. Cook, Lewisburg, Tennessee; my grandson.

- James M. Collins, Oct. 30, 1864 – Jan. 26, 1896
- William L. Collins, July 3, 1834 – Nov. 2, 1895
- Mary Jane Bickley, Sept. 21, 1844 – Apr. 1, 1877
- Sallie Carson, Sept. 15, 1842 – Aug. 21, 1895
- Arch C., son of A.B. and Mollie Collins, Sept. 19, 1904 – Nov. 2, 1904
- N.J. Mann, daughter John and Sallie Lipscomb, July 17, 1832 – Dec. 29, 1895
- Robert Newton Mann, Mar. 1, 1825 – Nov. 23, 1903
- Henry Trall Mann, Dec. 5, 1872 – Dec. 23, 1891
- Lucy M. Dean Mosely, Jan. 26, 1824 – July 18, 1884
- Mary M. Lipscomb, Nov. 24, 1838 – Apr. 8, 1871
- H.B. and A.H. Moore (infant son) died Sept. 16, 1868
- William C. Lipscomb, June 7, 1801 – Dec. 20, 1877

Appendix I

- Elizabeth Lipscomb, Feb. 23, 1808 – March 16, 1847 (also four infants)
- William Lipscomb, Jan. 17, 1771 – Jan. 17, 1829
- Ann D. Cook Lipscomb, Aug. 8, 1779 – March 26, 1870
- Garland N. Mann, Apr. 29, 1865 – May 21, 1866
- Mary F. Mann, Age 22, Died June 16, 1882
- Manse Diffie and Mother (Unmarked)
- Uncle Wm. Church (Unmarked)
- Several stone covered graves (Unnamed)

These names and information supplied by Mrs. Douglas W. Binns, 418 Sunnyside Drive, Nashville, sister of Mr. Fred Ralston, funeral director at Fayetteville.

- Kathleen Dillon Johnston, Died August 10, 1883
- John Calhoun Jones, Died about 1885
- Elinor Josephine Johnston Jones, Died June 20, 1892
- Several graves of colored people (Unmarked)
- Fred Scheffler (Unmarked)

Buy the Truth and Sell it Not:
The Life of E. Gaston Collins

The digital edition contains the full text, endnotes, and bibliography. The print editions also contain 130 illustrations and 9 appendices.

Available from booksellers everywhere.

Published by:
Unclouded Press
Lewisburg, Tennessee

www.uncloudedpress.com

e-mail: uncloudedpress@gmail.com

www.ingramcontent.com/pod-product-compliance
Lightning Source LLC
Chambersburg PA
CBHW051941290426
44110CB00015B/2069